Boatyards
& Marinas

Boatyards & Marinas

A Boat Owner's Guide to Smart Shopping

―――――

Ralph Naranjo

―――――

International Marine Publishing Company
Camden, Maine

Published by International Marine Publishing Co., a division of Highmark Publishing Ltd., Route 1, P.O. Box 220, Camden, Maine 04843.

Typeset by Farrar Associates, White Horse Beach, MA
Printed and bound by BookCrafters, Chelsea, MI
Designed by Abby Trudeau

10 9 8 7 6 5 4 3 2 1

LIBRARY OF CONGRESS
Library of Congress Cataloging-in-Publication Data

Naranjo, Ralph J.
  Boatyards and marinas : a boat owner's guide to smart shopping / Ralph Naranjo.
      p.   cm.
  Includes index.
  ISBN 0-87742-962-6 : $17.95
  1. Boatyards.   2. Marinas.   I. Title.
VM321.5.N37 1988   88-21070
627'.38—dc19   CIP

TO BOB MELROSE

Sailor—Boatyard Advocate—Friend

Contents

Preface

BOATYARDS AND MARINAS PLAY a significant role in the life of most boat owners. To some folks, such marine facilities represent frustrations, exorbitant expenses, and unmet commitments. Other owners see just the opposite. They relate well to the professionals who assist them in deriving more from their recreational boating time. I have written this book for both advocates and adversaries. It focuses on the technical and financial, as well as the political and social, aspects involved in where you keep your boat.

As a 12-year-old boy, I often listened to the wisdom of Captain Russwood Muff, a local clam digger/philosopher who lived in a beached houseboat. From this shoreside dwelling he rented skiffs, leased mooring rights (which he had taken upon himself to oversee), and assumed the role of resident boatwright. He afforded me a rather casual introduction to the marine business. One afternoon, I watched him attempt to start a Johnson Seahorse outboard motor. After 15 minutes of perspiration and salty dialogue, Captain Muff bent over, loosened the transom bracket clamps and sent the Seahorse to its last corral. I was impressed by such decisiveness.

Today, waterfront personalities have changed and outboard motors are reputed to be more reliable. Over the last 30 years, the marine industry has matured. Entrepreneurs realized that a market existed for professional services and products that could be sold at prices competitive with other industries. Most waterfronts have been renovated, and the boat owner has clearly achieved full consumer status.

As a sailor who runs a boatyard, I get to see both sides of the fence. During the past six years, I have been involved with the development of a full-service boatyard and waterfront operation. Prior to that, my family and I spent five years crossing three great oceans. In New Zealand, we hauled our sloop, *Wind Shadow*, at Salthouse Brothers Boatyard. Here we went through a major "do-it-yourself" refit and I began to consider the idea of turning a lifelong boating involvement into a vocation. This combination of vantage points—sailor, boat owner, craftsman and yard manager—has added, I hope, an important perspective to this book. I understand the groans of a client looking at the cost of replacing his sloop's 25 h.p. diesel. I am also all too familiar with the economic factors that have caused prices to reach so high.

Powerboat owners have more in common with sailors than many realize. This is especially true when it comes to choosing the right boatyard. Over the years I have run a yard which services about ten times as many sailboats as powerboats. Even so, we find that most skills needed to provide quality maintenance and refit work are directly transferable. Mechanics like the larger engine rooms and well-organized equipment often associated with power-boats. Carpenters, fiberglassers, and painters look at surfaces, not philosophies toward going to sea. In short, although this book has been written primarily with sailboats in mind, most of the material is equally applicable to powerboats, and I have tried to be inclusive.

Boatyards and Marinas focuses on cost-effective recommendations for the boat owner and is based upon valuable insights from professionals. Research for this book includes surveys of operations, personal interviews, and visits to yards varying in size from two-man operations to facilities issuing more than 100 paychecks weekly. This book will explain how to find the right boatyard or marina, and what to do once you have made the choice.

1

What Kind of Boatyard Are You Looking For?

P HYLLIS AND FRANK CLEARY think they are examples of cost-effective boat owners. Frank is a C.P.A. who
has revolutionized the accounting procedures of many a small
business. Through data processing, Frank has found ways to add
detail to even the most minute of details. During one gray winter he
wrote a software program that allowed him to track all of his
boating expenditures. It provided spreadsheet summaries with a
myriad of vital statistics. For example, he was able to compare the
cost and weight of antifouling bottom paint, and cross-reference
this with the number of barnacles discovered at the end of the
season. He could account for every foam brush, inch of masking
tape, and drop of Boat Soap used annually. In short, he had
boating cost factors in the palm of his hand.

When it came time to make a decision about where to haul his
sloop *Bottom Line*, Frank turned to his personal computer and
began to enter the data. He entered storage prices, labor rates, and
the contract details of each yard he was considering. Hidden costs
did not elude his scrutiny. He noted the extra charge for bottom
cleaning, the additional mast storage fee, and the mandatory
bottom painting and topside waxing, mentioned in fine print.
Frank knew his data base was pure.

And that was why he found it so difficult to accept that the yard
chosen by his computer had not worked out at all. He had reviewed
the statistics so carefully. Budget Marine had been a clear winner.

Seawanhaka Corinthian Yacht Club and Boatyard (Oyster Bay, New York), the author's home yard.

Cost projections were 6.315% lower than the next closest competitor and 8.792% lower than both the arithmetic mean and mode for the 12 yards Frank surveyed. Nevertheless, it was true; his yard expenditures had risen more than in previous years and the work accomplished just didn't meet his expectations. How could such empirically accurate data be so wrong? The answer is worth serious consideration.

"Don't make pricing your sole criterion for choosing a boatyard," warns Thomas Hale, past president of the American Boat Builders and Repairers Association, and a 25-year veteran of the industry. Tom's statement, timely advice in its own right, also illuminates the major flaw in Frank's calculations—the fact that cost analysis is only one side of a very multisided issue. "Cost-effective boatyarding" does not necessarily mean going with the lowest bid. Those who go with the cheapest estimates usually learn expensive lessons. When it comes to boat handling and maintenance, several factors precede dollar signs.

State of the art facility in Florida. (Hatteras, Fort Lauderdale)

YOUR TIME AND MONEY

Do-it-yourself efforts can significantly reduce upkeep costs, and a boatyard that permits, or even encourages, owner maintenance can prove to be a real bargain. Before embarking on the parsimonious path to budget haulouts though, we must touch on one crucial issue. It has to do with the relationship between money and time. Owners must determine how much of each they are willing—and able—to invest in their craft. It's true, in a sense, that the more time one has available to perform boat maintenance, the fewer dollars need be spent. But whether this amounts to cost effectiveness is another story altogether.

Beware of the amateur's worst pitfall, inefficiency. A friend once boasted to me about how much money he saved changing the oil and filter on his sloop's auxiliary engine. When asked how long this took, his wife responded, "All weekend." On Friday afternoon he pumped out the old oil with a leaky hand pump. After cleaning the bilge, wiping down the sides of the engine room compartment, and changing his clothes, he discovered that his filter wrench refused to grip the oil filter. On Saturday morning he delayed his weekend cruise and went off to purchase the proper filter wrench. Three hardware stores later he was back at the boat, confident of success. The filter twisted loose, and oil again found its way into the bilge. The new filter was difficult to hold in place and the threads were marred; my friend spent another hour and a half coaxing it onto the stud. The bilge again needed cleaning but the cruise was scheduled to begin. The engine started without hesitation, but shortly after the harbor jetties were left astern, an acrid odor filled the cabin. A quick look in the engine room revealed a mist of heated lubricating oil, the result of a leak dripping onto the exhaust manifold. The engine was shut down and the crew sailed back into the marina.

Once alongside, my friend went into the engine room to troubleshoot the situation. For the third time, he cleaned oil from places where it did not belong. After consulting the marina's dockmaster my friend determined he hadn't wet the filter gasket with oil prior to screwing on the filter. The dry surface and his overly enthusiastic tightening combined to tear the gasket from its properly seated position. By midday Sunday my friend had found another filter, installed it properly, and again mopped the bilge clean of spilled oil. His do-it-yourself money-saver took 11½ hours to accomplish, caused the cancellation of his weekend cruise, and consumed every paper towel on board. A professional would have completed the job in an hour, and threatened neither the weekend cruise nor the wellbeing of the engine.

Although this is an extreme—but hardly atypical—story, other examples of inefficiency versus cost effectiveness are easy to find. For example, each spring boat bottoms are sanded, prepared, and painted. Some yards insist that their staff do the work. Others allow owners the option of tackling the task themselves. Specialized electric and pneumatic sanders allow the skilled professional to keep prep time to a minimum. Product knowledge and application skills also reduce the pro's painting time. It's not unusual to discover that yard employees can do a better job in half the time it takes the boat owner to complete the same task. This means that the owner is not effectively swapping one of his own hours of labor for one that the yard sells. In the hypothetical bottom painting situation, the reduced quality of the results and the time taken to complete the job equates to a two-to-one disparity between pro and amateur labor. In the case of the oil change mentioned earlier, the ratio approaches ten to one.

If you enjoy maintenance, that's a different story. All repetitive maintenance tasks benefit from a learning curve, and time and repetition bring to some serious amateurs skills that a pro might envy. But if maintenance feels like drudgery to be endured rather than a pleasure to be enjoyed, then you need to keep a careful accounting. Calculate the hours spent doing each refit task and translate the figure into yard labor dollars. This will give a realistic picture of what your time is actually worth. My friend's efforts to change the oil gave his labor a value equivalent to the 1962 minimum wage. If he wanted to be cost effective, he should have had the boatyard do the work, and spent two extra hours at his job earning an overtime wage. He would have come out way ahead.

Here is good advice for the boat owner who doesn't like to roll up his sleeves and get into the details of his vessel's maintenance or refit: Put quality personnel at the top of your priority list. The nitty-gritty of how to find a quality operation will be detailed in the next chapter, but as a simple answer, the results of quality can be seen in the yard itself. A yard is usually known for its engine work, carpentry, painting skills, or fiberglass repair work, and its reputation is linked to the satisfied customers who have had work done and are pleased with the results. For better or worse, it is part of the conversation in yacht club bars and trains on the way to work, so ask questions of other boat owners. And if you become interested in a specific facility, don't be afraid to stop by, introduce yourself, and have a look at what is going on. The operations with the better reputations have usually come by them honestly.

Ideally, you should look for a yard where both you and your boat can develop a long-term relationship. The better a pro gets to know a vessel and the systems aboard, the more effective the

World voyager Dave Martin appreciates a yard where he can shoulder a large part of the maintenance himself.

If you don't enjoy maintenance chores, put quality personnel at the top of your list.

maintenance program becomes. Those boat owners who hop from yard to yard chasing low bid estimates usually discover they lose the allegiance of the personnel and don't save money in the long run. A boatyard is like a community: the more involved you become, the more you can derive from it.

FALSE SAVINGS

One of the key traits shared among cost-conscious boaters is the ability to explore frugal alternatives. Sometimes these can work, and work very well. I have seen examples of owners successfully banding together to operate their own haulout facility and others who effectively combine a winter cruise with cheaper storage and repair facilities in the South, or foreign ports. But I have heard plenty of horror stories as well.

Several years ago, friends of ours seemed to have found an ideal boat storage alternative. They lived in the Northeast but decided to keep their boat in Florida. The yard where they chose to store their vessel and have its maintenance performed was well run, and because of the region's lower labor costs, quality craftsmanship was available at bargain prices. It all seemed too good to be true.

Their perspective changed after a single phone call from the boatyard. They were informed that their boat had been broken into and much of their gear was missing. Upon arrival in Florida, the owners discovered that, in fact, everything from the autopilot to the Zodiak had been taken. They did have insurance coverage, and it eventually compensated them for most of what was taken. But it didn't cover the time involved in re-outfitting an extensively equipped vessel. Nor did it fully compensate them for the cosmetic damage done to the boat. Our friends learned a tough lesson about boatyard security.

Where you leave your vessel, and who is in charge of it, can be very important. High crime rate areas should be avoided regardless of how skilled the craftsmen are. Tall fences and guard dogs tend to indicate a problem rather than guarantee sensible protection from it. There are a variety of alarm systems and locks on the market. However, I would prefer to find another spot rather than fortify against such a situation.

It is also important to keep in mind that a boat is a heavy, cumbersome, and fragile object, and in the equipment required to haul, move, and store it, one is dealing with some formidable physical forces. It surely is a false economy to seek a bargain that threatens the safety of the boat or its crew. Beware of bargain boatyards with old, poorly maintained equipment, or equipment of correct design but inappropriate size. In one instance I know of, a yard attempted to haul a 42-foot cruising ketch using one of those small vehicular cranes. The crane was in good shape but undersized for the job, and the operator, who was not trained in the use of heavy equipment, was operating the crane beyond the limits of its rated capacity. The boat was too heavy to be lifted and moved with the crane's outriggers up, so the operator planned to lift the boat with the outriggers down, then rotate the crane's boom to move the vessel. In order to keep the load distance from center as

Old, tired cranes can be a gamble.

short as possible, the crane made its way along the very edge of a small, earth-filled pier. Its outriggers were placed on railroad ties that made up the pier's outside edging. Apparently no one checked to see whether these ties were properly fastened. When the boat was lifted, the pier's structural bulkhead failed and the crane outriggers lost their support. The boat listed to starboard, and the boom of the toppling crane came down like a guillotine, amputating the forward third of the vessel. Fortunately, no one was killed and the boat was eventually rebuilt. The disaster underscores the danger of using equipment in a manner for which it was not intended.

The boat owner is not a heavy equipment specialist, so evaluating the suitability of a crane or other hauling equipment presents some complications. But don't learn by trial and error. I would never want my boat to be the heavyweight waiting to test an unknown piece of equipment. A consumer looking only for the lowest rates may be enticed by the facilities with the worst equipment. Non-existent maintenance programs and minimum capital expenditures help such facilities keep down overhead. Don't wait to discover that the wire cable on the crane hauling your boat was on the 25-year-old machine when it left the factory. A systematic procedure for evaluating boatyard equipment will be detailed in the next chapter, but some dangers are obvious. It doesn't require technical expertise to detect that a frayed, thread-bare set of lifting slings needs replacement. Nor is it difficult to identify a tired marine railway with its worn, worm-eaten ties, and cars that tend to jump off the rusty track.

DEVELOPING TRUST

As a professional in the industry, I must underscore the fact that most boatyards are reputable operations where you will get what you pay for. In preparing this book, I made a survey of some 25 boatyards, mostly clustered in the Northeast, but with representation from coast to coast. Specifics will be detailed throughout the book, but here I would like to say a bit about the overwhelming consensus. Time and time again one word seemed to appear in the responses to my questionnaire. "Communication" was the key issue of nearly every yard manager. As Richard Egan, at the Crosby Yacht Yard in Massachusetts says, "Communication helps the customer to understand the boatyard's problems, and the yard to understand what the customer expects and can afford."

Trust was another often mentioned concern. Charlie Beaumont, at Mystic Shipyard in Connecticut, states, "Boat owners need to assume a yard is honest until proven otherwise." If you approach a yard with an adversarial attitude, you are starting out with the wrong foot forward. Negative attitudes are contagious and have sealed the fate of many boatyard/owner relationships. Lee Austin, at Marathon Boatyard in Florida, says harmony exists where there

BOATYARD SURVEY
The following individuals and boatyards participated in the survey. Their interest and efforts are much appreciated.

State	Boatyard	Respondent
California	Anacapa Marine	Gil Macquire
Maine	Brooklin Boatyard, Inc.	Steve White
Connecticut	Crocker's Boatyard	Dave Crocker
Massachusetts	Crosby Yacht Yard, Inc.	Richard Egan
Florida	Derecktor Gunnell	James Brewer
Connecticut	Dodson Boat Yard	R. J. Snyder
Connecticut	Essex Boat Works	Stu Ingersoll
Massachusetts	Falmouth Marine, Inc.	Robert M. Ackland
Maryland	Georgetown Yacht Basin, Inc.	Phil Parish
Maine	Henry R. Hinckley	Ti Hack
New York	International Marine	Bob Heese
Rhode Island	Jamestown Boat Yard	Jano Billings
Florida	Marathon Boatyard, Inc.	Lee Austin
Massachusetts	Martha's Vineyard Shipyard	Philip Hale
Massachusetts	Mattapoisett Boatyard, Inc.	Arthur W. McLean
New York	Melrose Marine	Bob Melrose
Washington	Miller & Miller	Paul Miller
Connecticut	Mystic Shipyard, Inc.	Charlie Beaumont
Massachusetts	Onset Bay Marina, Inc.	Skip Robinson
Connecticut	Pilot's Point Marina	Rives Potts
Maine	Wayfarer Marine Corp.	Stuart Farnham
Rhode Island	Williams & Manchester	Tom Rich
Connecticut	Yacht Haven	Lee Frantz
Maryland	Zahniser's Sailing Ctr.	A. W. Zahniser

is "a good job for a fair price, quality employees, and knowledgeable boat owners." The foundation for such relationships begins with dialogue. Steve White, at Brooklin Boatyard in Maine, likes to see "knowledgeable owners who will ask for advice and then listen to what is said." He also adds, "Comparing boatyards can be like comparing oranges and watermelons, with as many solutions to problems as there are yards." Through trust and communication these variables can be handled, and the boat owner, his vessel, and the boatyard can thrive. And this, in the long run, will nearly always turn out to be the most cost-effective option.

AMBIENCE

A final point, which has little to do with cost effectiveness, may have everything to do with long run customer satisfaction. The right boatyard must have a certain ambience. For some it means simplicity. They like the feeling of a wood burning stove and trust the chaps who run the marine railway. Others seek technology's cutting edge. They need a facility that provides spray refinishing,

This well-lit, well-equipped boatshop retains a traditional ambience.

refrigeration, air conditioning repairs, as well as maintenance for their vessel's satellite communication equipment. Decide for yourself what your needs are, and what style is comfortable. Listen to your subjective side. Personal impressions often count for more than paperbound statistics. Sailing is a pleasurable experience, and your vessel is more than an expensive aggregate of materials needing constant maintenance. It is important to choose a yard with which you, as well as your boat, are in harmony.

2

The Modern Boatyard

———————

E QUIPMENT IS ONE OF the key issues in today's boatyards. Technology has certainly had an impact on how boats
are hauled, stored, maintained, and repaired, and better boat-
handling gear and labor-saving tools have greatly increased the
industry's efficiency. As a boating consumer, you need to be aware
of these innovations in hardware. That doesn't mean that you have
to know how to run a travelift, but you should certainly understand
the advantages that contemporary equipment offers. A close look
at the gear involved and how it is handled and maintained can also
tell you a lot about the yard under consideration.

HAULOUT EQUIPMENT

Marine Railways

Today the old standby known as the marine railway is on its way to
becoming an endangered species, although it is still a widely
available alternative. The hauling process includes placing a vessel
in a cradle, soundly secured to a railway carriage, which rides on an
iron track arrangement. In areas with a large tidal range, a vessel
can be moved into the supports at high tide; later, at low water, it
can be thoroughly checked and reblocked in preparation for the
steep ride up the beach. A large winch handles a cable or chain
attached to the railway carriage, providing the energy to traverse

the incline. Once ashore, the boat is moved around the yard by a yard truck, by a further series of winches and cables, or in some operations, by a switch track system.

One of the reasons the marine railway is becoming outmoded is because of its labor-intensive nature. In boatyards, as in other industries, labor costs have skyrocketed. A modern mobile lift can haul a 50-foot sloop in less than a half hour and quickly move it to its storage location, all in one operation. If a marine railway system were used, the man-hours involved might be tripled or quadrupled.

Nevertheless, the traditional marine railway remains a viable boat handling alternative. This is especially true where capital is not available for pier building and travelift purchase. Haulouts take more man-hours to execute, but they can be safely carried out. I would much rather trust my own sloop to an aging railway than a cable crane of similar vintage. As with any piece of boatyard equipment, maintenance and skillful handling go a long way toward extending the gear's useful lifespan.

It is essential that a marine railway system be based on a sound support structure. Most marine railways rely on timber ties for the support of the tracks themselves, and rotten ties are a serious—and all too common—problem. Creosote-treated and pressure-treated timbers are gaining in popularity, and it's not uncommon to find ties wrapped in plastic, securely fastened with Monel staples. Keeping oxygen away from the wood tends to retard the growth of marine organisms. Replacing underwater railway ties is a labor-intensive project, and hence, frequently postponed. A concerned boat owner should use a spring low tide to get a look at railway ties normally underwater.

Marine railways are based on a pounds (or tons)- per-foot measurement. This means that a facility that can haul a long 1,200-ton cargo vessel might not be able to haul a relatively short 500-ton tug. The distance over which the load is spread is as important as the weight itself. In large marine railway structures the iron track is placed on wooden bearers called rails. Cross cap ties often have pilings driven to refusal beneath them. Lighter-duty yacht-type railways (for vessels weighing less than 25 tons) frequently eliminate the pilings and the timber rails: they simply span each cross tie with two iron tracks. Deflection between spans can be a problem, and a wise owner carefully watches vessels heavier than his own being hauled.

The optimum width between ties varies according to the application. A backyard boatyard may get away with hauling a light 30-footer on well-maintained tracks only five to six feet wide. Most commercial marine railways are eight feet or wider. The important concern here is that the wider the span, the stronger the midsection of the railway carriage must be. This structure is usually a welded metal frame soundly attached to the flanged wheels that ride on the track. In some cases, there are adjustable uprights, moved in and out to accommodate various hull shapes. In other situations, cradles are secured to the carriage and removed once they reach the top of the incline. In this latter case, there should be a positive means of lashing or locking the cradle to the carriage.

Quite a bit of energy must be exerted on the carriage, cradle, and vessel to coax them up an incline. Some yards use block and tackle arrangements, while others rely upon reduction gearing and a stout winch mechanism. The key factor is the quality of all components involved. Worn or undersized blocks can explode, with lethal results. If a rusty cable separates, a controlled haulout can quickly turn into a hasty launching.

To distribute the hauling loads effectively, it is important that the hauling cable attachment point be well engineered, not simply a line tied about the cradle. I prefer to see a large wire reel winch that does not require direct handling. The wire rope needs to be regularly oiled. A few operations wisely drag the cable through an oil trough just ahead of the spool as each boat is pulled up the beach face.

Careful attention to the foregoing points should help you determine whether a given marine railway is up to the job of handling your boat. The rest depends on the skill of the haulout crew. Watch several boats being hauled to see if the following concerns are addressed:

- Vessels are of an appropriate draft and displacement for the capacity of the railway.

- Wind, sea, and tidal factors are considered, so that vessels are brought smoothly into their cradles.
- Cradle is securely fastened to the railway carriage.
- Vessel is properly positioned and well secured in the cradle.
- Cable is running clear, and yard personnel stand out of its way.

Travelifts and Cranes

You may have noticed that I have taken the liberty of using the term *travelift* to refer to all mobile sling lifts. These units, derivatives of the original, rail-bound Algonac Hoists, have revolutionized the container shipping industry as well as the majority of boatyards, and have earned the distinction of being the most important single piece of equipment in many boatyards. In addition to the lifts manufactured by Marine Travelift, Inc., other reliable brand names include Acme Lift, Tami Lift, and others.

For the boat owner, however, the biggest concern is not who made the equipment, but rather, how it is maintained and operated. During your perusal of a yard or marina, inquire about the rated capacity of the lift. Take a walk around it and look at the tires. They are usually recapped aircraft tires, and the sidewalls should be checked for excessive wear and tear. Then look at the slings; they should be unfrayed, clean, and attached to the cable blocks with appropriate hardware. Examine closely to see if all the large clevis pins are secured with appropriate cotter pins or quick-slip pins. Make sure the main lifting cables are in good shape. Many yards do not oil or grease the wire because of cosmetic problems with residue landing on decks. This is an acceptable approach as long as the yard is ready to replace the wire rope at intervals much shorter than if it had been kept well oiled.

Conclude your casual inspection with an overview of the unit. Does it look well maintained? Has it been kept painted or allowed to rust? Are there signs of leaking hydraulic fluid or lubricating oil? Although you may not have a clue how the travelift is operated, you probably can get a pretty good idea of how it has been treated.

Mobile swing lifts, such as the Marine Travelift depicted here, have revolutionized the haulout operation and have earned the distinction of being the most valuable single piece of equipment in many boatyards.

Mobile lifts handle both sailboats and powerboats easily. (Cove Haven, Barrington, Rhode Island)

Lift tires are often recapped aircraft tires. Check sidewalls for excessive wear and tear.

Be sure that the sling stitching is in good condition.

Powerful hydraulic cranes are a valuable boatyard tool.

While there are exceptions, it usually holds true that those who neglect their own equipment are not going to treat your vessel much differently.

In many areas, large hydraulic and mechanical cranes are popular. Once again, sound, well-maintained equipment of appropriate size is of primary importance. Beware if your vessel is 20–30% larger than anything else in the yard. There is something nervewracking about knowing that your boat is the annual cable tester.

Several years ago, while cruising with my family along the Australian coast, we ran across cruising friends during a brief layover, whose most recent experiences astounded us. More than a year before, they had sailed their stout wooden ketch, *Betty Lou,* into a small coastal harbor and had arranged for a haulout at a local boatyard. The staff of the yard used a cable crane equipped with slings to haul the vessel. All appeared secure as *Betty Lou* was lifted out of the water. The next moment, there was the gunshot

Mechanical crane in action. Long cables are better than short ones, but the best solution is a crane with a spreader box (right) *which keeps the sling from compressing the hull-to-deck joint.*

sound of the boom support cable parting, and the ketch plunged back into the water. The crane's steel boom came crashing down onto the vessel, just forward of the companionway. The situation was worsened by the fact that one of our friends was aboard. The haulout crew had failed to insist that no one be aboard while the vessel was being hauled. The impact seriously injured our friend, destroyed the couple's vessel, and ended their voyage. The yard took the view that the incident was "an act of God." The result was that our friends had to remain in the area for two years in order to secure a settlement through the Australian legal system.

This tragic episode underscores several important concerns. First is the issue of safety. Manufacturers of hauling equipment stress that no one should be aboard a boat being hauled. Boatyard personnel are aware of the potential hazards and normally prevent such situations from occurring. The owner of the facility in which this accident took place also had alluded to the fact that he didn't

Crane haulout with slings correctly positioned to distribute the load while avoiding the knotmeter impeller. But note the compression loading on the hull-to-deck joint.

really have an accurate idea of how much the timber ketch weighed. It is often surprising to discover the degree of variation in displacement among vessels of similar overall length. When cruising gear and provisions are loaded aboard a boat, the total weight dramatically increases. A heavy-displacement, blue water equipped, 40-footer can weigh twice as much as its modern, 'round-the-buoys' counterpart. The professional in charge of overseeing haulouts should be able to recognize the difference between the heavyweights and the flyweights. The owner, meanwhile, should know roughly what his or her vessel weighs in its current trim and pass this information on to the yard foreman or manager.

Whether your boat is being hauled by crane or by lift, sling placement is essential to a safe haulout. The operator of the lift must be familiar with the configuration of a vessel's underbody, know whether or not there are knotmeter impellers in the way, and also be certain he is not placing the lifting slings on the prop, shaft, strut, or edge of the keel. Some manufacturers place sling location marks on a vessel's side deck. In situations where there remains a

X-shaped spreader box allows boats to be crane-hoisted with spars still in place.

Sling placement is an important concern. Note how the angle of the bow sling acts to prevent slippage. The stern sling is placed carefully to avoid propeller/rudder interface.

question, many professionals find value in a profile plan, a long boathook with which to probe an underbody, or even a swim with a face mask to get a closer look.

Theoretically, the weight of a boat should be evenly distributed between the straps. In practice, boat positioning usually results in some minor variations. In most cases the cables attached to the sling straps should angle inward toward the blocks on the travelift. This helps to counteract any tendency for the slings to slip toward the ends of the boat. Occasionally vessels with extreme rocker or other limiting design features require that the slings be tied together in order to prevent dangerous slippage. The accompanying illustration shows the correct geometry for a safe haulout.

When observing a professional haulout operation, pay heed to the little things. Watch how the crew gets the vessel into the U-shaped lifting piers: do they use a push boat or the boat's own engine? Do they seem comfortable with either alternative? Notice how the need for lines or fenders is handled. When a vessel with a

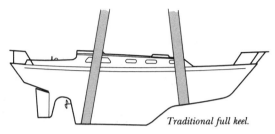

Traditional full keel.

Keep slings clear of transducers, fragile trailing edges of keels, and rudder and propeller shafts.

Headstay may need removal in order to position. Be sure deck-stepped mast is adequately supported.

Safety line may also be used to prevent slippage.

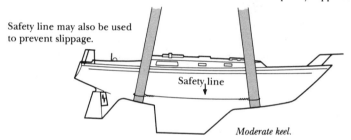

Safety line

Moderate keel.

Lifting slings angled to prevent slippage toward end of vessel.

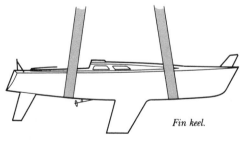

Fin keel.

Often a 90° angle at the sling-to-hull contact point makes the most effective anti-slip alternative. Avoid steeply sloping keel/hull intersections.

Typical sling placement for various hull configurations. (Jim Sollers illustration)

Covering lift slings with tubular plastic protects boats as well as slings.

roller-furling headstay is brought into the lifting slip, the haulout crew should skillfully prevent the extruded foil from colliding with the crossbeam at the leading end of the lift. Quite often the headstay must be detached to ensure clearance as the vessel is hoisted out of the water. If the mast is deck-stepped (often indicated by the lack of a mast boot), observe how the yard staff approaches the issue of releasing the headstay. Do they leave an open fore-triangle and simply rely upon the shrouds to keep the spar in the boat, or do they take a more conservative approach and secure a halyard to a sound attachment point on the foredeck somewhat aft of the stem? Little things like this can make a big difference, and it is not too difficult to determine whether or not a crew knows what it's doing.

Checking the Hauling Platform

Each piece of hauling equipment utilizes some form of platform from which to provide its service. The integrity of the supporting structure is as important as the mechanical reliability of the lifting

Jib boom for hauling masts. The well-fendered float is a reassuring sign that this yard pays attention to detail.

A well-designed dual travelift pier at Pilot's Point Marina (Westbrook, Connecticut), featuring steel H-beam runways.

mechanism itself. Most travelifts move out over open water via a piling-supported or earth-filled bulkhead structure. The compression loads imposed upon these piers are a sum of the equipment weight plus the total displacement of the vessel. Good travelift pier design dictates the use of steel H-beam runways to spread the loads evenly across the tops of the pilings. The use of one vertical pile, with an inclined batter pile on the outboard side further stabilizes the construction (see accompanying photo). Pressure-treated lumber or creosote-dipped timber greatly adds to the longevity of the structure. A conventional timber piling driven to refusal (i.e., to the point where each strike of the slide hammer results in less than 1/2 inch of further movement into the substrate) will normally support a compression load of 20,000 pounds. After years of attack by marine organisms, ice, and wood rot that number changes drastically. Most boatyard professionals know the signs of deterioration; unfortunately, a few don't always heed the warning.

A bulkheaded, back-filled structure endures the same compression loads as a piling pier, but is designed to spread the

Notice the tie rods and batter piles (right) *in this well-built pier.*

downward moment of force safely into the substrate. Occasionally a builder forgets about the intertidal hydrostatic effect of sea water as it rushes into and out of the structure. As we saw in the preceding chapter, a poorly supported sea wall, lacking crossbracing, tie-rods, or deadmen piles, can give way under the heavy load of a crane lifting someone's treasured sloop. Be sure that both the lift and the surface it is operated on are up to the task of handling your vessel. For your own peace of mind take a close look at what is used to support the yard's travelift before it hoists your vessel from the water.

Innovators

The Brownell Boat Works company manufactures a line of truly unique trailers capable of being submerged on conventional ramp runways. Through the use of remote controls, hydraulically operated support arms are raised and lowered. This allows a vessel to be hauled from the water and transported across the yard—or across the country—with no further handling. This piece of gear

A Brownell haulout. This ingenious hydraulic trailer makes it possible to haul even a very large keel boat on any ramp runway. Once hauled, the boat can be moved across the yard—or across the country.

A well-built cradle is essential for over-the-road transport.

Rob Lee, Vice-President of Sea and Land Design, Inc., standing next to his firm's "Yard Boss." This self-propelled hydraulic cradle greatly expedites boat handling.

has opened up new growth in the alternate storage market. Many vessels are being delivered to personal residences or boatyards many miles from more costly shoreside facilities.

Other companies, such as Sea and Land Design, Inc., also manufacture labor-saving boat handling gear. The "Yard Boss" is a self-propelled hydraulic cradle that greatly expedites boat handling. The unit is, basically, an open-ended trailer with a frame bed that can be raised and lowered about 12 inches. In addition to the up-and-down lift capability of the bed, the unit has three pairs of hydraulically controlled support arms, which can control the boat laterally. These adjustable arms can be quickly positioned to support just about any configuration of a sailboat or powerboat hull. The entire trailer is propelled by a pair of hydraulically driven wheels. These are designed to maneuver the vehicle in tight confines, which allows the maximum use of limited areas. Once a boat is in its storage space and blocked up with jack stands, the open-ended mobile cradle pulls away, ready to pick up another boat.

BLOCKING

Boats are designed to float, not stand in a boatyard. When a boat is on land, both lateral and fore-and-aft stability depend on the system of supports connecting the hull to terra firma. The narrow-base, fin keel sailboats in vogue nowadays make propping up a vessel somewhat like standing a triangle on end. The only thing working in the boat's favor is the fact that its center of gravity is low.

Wooden cradles, steel jack stands, and a variety of equivalent devices can be used to provide stability, but each system must be tailored to fit the individual boat. Those who are responsible for this phase of the boatyard operation have to keep in mind meteorological factors as well as engineering constraints. In some areas, seasonal gales can create a serious test of the effectiveness of any blocking system. When you are looking over a yard's storage techniques, remember that no vessel has ever fallen over because it was too well supported.

Cradles and jack stands are the two most popular means of blocking in use today.

The yard staff must understand where stresses, caused by the weight of the vessel, are being focused. Many new travelifts have load-cell gauges that give an accurate reading of the weight each sling is supporting. But the crew needs to be aware of more than just the displacement of a vessel. Factors such as hull construction and the shape and structure of the keel are vitally important in determining the type of blocking needed and the way in which a boat is transferred to its blocking. For example, some internal ballast fin keels have a very fine trailing edge, which is not only the deepest point of draft but also one of the hull's most fragile areas. If the full weight of the vessel is transferred to this point, the glass laminate can be crushed and major structural damages incurred. When on land, this type of keel needs to have its load spread over as wide an area as possible. The blocking crew usually accomplishes this by building a base of support timbers. The load is gradually eased onto this support structure, as the yard staff checks to avoid excessive point loading (concentrating all the weight at one point).

A deep draft fin keel sailboat makes propping up a vessel something like standing a triangle on end.

A travelift load-cell gauge measures the amount of weight each sling is supporting.

If your boat has an encapsulated ballast fin keel with a V-shaped cross section at the foot, be sure to mention this to the yard manager at the time you are making hauling arrangements. These are important factors affecting how the vessel will be blocked up. External lead or iron ballast can withstand the effects of point loading more easily than relatively fragile fiberglass laminates.

Incorrectly built or adjusted cradles are another cause for concern, particularly when dealing with thin-skinned fiberglass production boats. Their lack of flexural strength makes them extremely vulnerable to point loading, and serious problems may arise in situations where hull pads touch before the keel is solidly supported. I've seen boats that have been so twisted out of shape from mediocre construction and improper blocking that their bulkheads have broken free and cabin doors refuse to open or close. Permanent indentations in the hull can mark where excessive pad pressure has existed. A smart yard crew recognizes these and other symptoms that warn of potential blocking difficulties. Overall construction scantlings, as well as keel configuration and structure, are at the top of their checklist.

Jack stands must be placed against flatter (non-rounded) sections of the hull.

Excessive pressure on a jack stand pad can indent the hull. Check regularly.

Currently most yards prefer jack stands to cradles. Advocates of jack stands feel these devices are quicker and easier to handle, far more versatile, and easier to store in the off season than cradles. The other problem with wood cradles is that hidden factors can cause big problems. For instance, the bottom stringers on cradles tend to rot from the middle of the timber outward. A wise owner, as well as the yard foreman, checks the wood with a knife or an ice pick. The surface may look fine, but the support base may be all but useless.

Some yards, especially the ones that move boats with hydraulic trailer rigs such as the Kleeco Lift, prefer well-fabricated metal cradles. Many manufacturers have fitted jack pad supports for such cradles, which allow them to adapt to a variety of vessels. With this system, boats can be placed much closer together—a significant advantage for the yard. A few yards continue to build wooden blocking structures around each vessel hauled. But even with a skilled carpenter, the time involved, and the cost of the wood used, far exceeds the cost of blocking a boat with jack stands.

Most yards prefer jack stands for ease and versatility.

Powerboats also are easy to block with jack stands.

Small hydraulic trailers give a yard additional boat handling flexibility.

Boat being hauled on a Kleeco Lift trailer.

Custom-built wood blocking, with vertical supports and crossbracing. Because of the high materials and labor costs, jack stands are usually a more cost-effective option.

Regardless of what blocking system is used, a properly supported boat stands vertical, with its waterline parallel to level ground. In this position the decks and cockpit drain unhindered. Nearly all of the weight should be deployed through the full length of the keel. Side supports are placed as far outboard as possible, taking into consideration the changes in hull contour. The ground the vessel has been placed on must be stable and clear so as not to interfere with the blocking efforts.

Remember that the cradle or system of jack stands supporting your boat is only as secure as the terrain upon which it has been placed. Poor drainage, unsurfaced, muddy substrates, and low-lying areas prone to flooding can lead to disasters. I have seen boatyards inundated by a 10-foot tidal increase resulting from a hurricane. Shallow-draft vessels floated off their supports and were blown into deeper draft vessels yet unaffected by the rising water. Such nightmares are categorized by insurance underwriters as "Acts of God," which may mean "not covered" by your own policy.

CLEANING AND FINISHING EQUIPMENT

While certainly not of such strategic importance as hauling and blocking equipment, labor-saving tools such as pressure water sprayers, air files, impact wrenches, and sandblasting equipment have found a variety of uses in the contemporary boatyard. A full, well-maintained tool locker is another important indicator of a well-run operation.

Pressure water sprayers have benefited both boatyards and boat owners in recent years. Boat bottoms can now be washed clean in a fraction of the time it would take a person with a brush. These machines can also spray chemical cleaners, and are even used with sand to do abrasive water blasting. An application for which they are misused is in cleaning teak decks. The water exits the nozzle of the sprayer at 2,000 pounds per square inch. It will quickly remove dirt and grime from a teak deck, but it will also loosen caulking and do irreversible damage to the teak itself. If the applicator is careful and maintains an even movement of the spray wand, a deck will survive the first treatment and look almost as good as new. After the second encounter with such a process the teak will start to look like celery and need to be sanded flat. Today's teak decks are laid over plywood or fiberglass and are normally not more than 3/8 inch thick. They're fastened by countersunk screws covered by bungs that may be only 1/4 inch thick. Thus, these decks can't endure too much sanding caused by episodes with a pressure sprayer.

The ways old coatings are removed as well as applied have changed dramatically in recent years because of other advances in equipment and abrasive technology. Years ago, coatings were removed with sandpaper or with a blow torch and a scraper. Today, there are electrical machines and pneumatic equipment to expedite the process. Operations that specialize in quality spray refinishing put great faith in multi-motion, air-powered, disk sanders. These units are light and effectively produce a fine finish. Companies such as 3M provide an arsenal of self-sticking abrasive pads to complement the use of such equipment.

Spray refinishing requires talented professionals, as well as

Pressure spray equipment makes a quick job of bottom cleaning.

Attacking bottom blisters with a disk sander.

specialized equipment. If a yard does a large volume of this type of work it will need an inside facility that is clean and well lit. The shop's compressor should have a dryer and filter system and twice the capacity needed to run the tools in normal use. A small facility, for example, can get away with a 30 c.f.m.(cubic feet per minute), 220- or 440-volt electric compressor. This size system is fine for a spray painter and can run a couple of air tools at the same time. But it is inadequate for sandblasting or supplying air to other locations throughout a yard. Larger facilities often have units capable of delivering several hundred cubic feet of air per minute.

If you are a fiberglass or wooden boat owner, beware of the yard that handles a lot of metal work. Sandblasting is a continuous necessity in refinishing or building steel boats. The grit tends to fly everywhere, and neighboring vessels will be constantly dusted with the residue. Some of the more conscientious facilities have special sheds where they blast, keeping the abrasive material where it belongs. Even so, the marriage between metal boats and boats built of other materials is a questionable one. You'll find choosing a yard

Inside facilities are essential for quality control when handling today's high tech spray coatings. In this well-equipped facility, the solar door adds heat as well as light.

that specializes in the material from which your boat is constructed is the best choice in the long run.

Beware as well of enthusiastic newcomers to the craft of linear polyurethane refinishing. The freelancer with a van, a 110-volt compressor, and a beat-up disk sander may have lower overhead than a good boatyard; he might be ready to spray your boat on the next calm day; but are you ready for the results? His attractive low estimate could fall into the "you get what you pay for" category. Before deciding whether or not your boat should be part of a semi-pro's learning curve, take a close look at his past accomplishments. If the price and the product seem equitable, check with the yard you will store your boat in to see if it allows such work to be done.

THE QUALITY OPERATION

Equipment quality and workplace organization often are fair indicators of what type of craftsmanship can be expected. When

Examples of a yard's painting skills—or lack of them—are often woefully apparent.

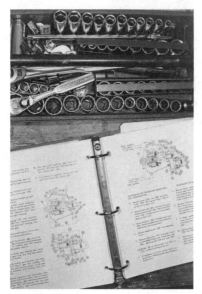

A well-organized, well-equipped shop with repair manuals ready to hand and a collection of essential specialized tools suggests a careful attention to detail.

you look over the shop facilities of a boatyard, pay attention to details. Notice whether or not the mechanic's tools are rusty and adrift on a bench that looks like it's been going to weather in a gale. Psychiatrists worry about compulsive organizers. Shop foremen develop ulcers over the opposite type of personality. Yes, quality mechanical work can evolve from a filthy corner, but it's certainly the exception rather than the rule.

Cosmetic concerns must be analyzed on an individual basis. Those who relate to gray paint rather than 10 coats of varnish may not be offended by a chap in work boots stepping onto a dorade box as he loosens a gooseneck fitting. Nor will they find fault with a few smears of blue bottom paint, originating from dirty, uncovered slings, appearing on their vessel's faded topsides. On the other hand, the owner of a gold plater testifying to expensive urethane technology will more than grimace at such thoughts. What is considered pampering in one yard may be standard practice in another. If the yard you are considering doesn't live up to your cosmetic expectations, give some thought to other alternatives.

Finally, despite the obvious advantages of a well-equipped operation, don't be misled into believing that a larger facility is always better than a smaller alternative. Our culture puts great faith in shiny hardware. We all too often subscribe to a philosophy based upon bigger being better. You shouldn't base judgment of a yard on its impressive array of equipment and technical surroundings and disregard the fact that it's the *people* whom you'll really count on. Quality is more contingent on the frame of mind of the craftsman than the brand of tools in his locker.

GUIDELINES FOR POWERBOATS

Powerboaters, like sailors, come with a wide range of outlooks and budgets. To be happy in a boatyard/marina situation, they, just like their wind-powered neighbors, must have confidence in the operation, enjoy their surroundings, and believe that they are getting what they pay for. Powerboaters looking for the right boatyard should follow nine-tenths of the guidelines given the sailboat owner. Obviously, disregard the hints about ballast keels, spars, and rigging. Focus on the mechanical abilities of the yard in question. Listen closely to the evaluations of those with similar boats or sisterships.

A powerboat has a need denoted by its name: engine reliability is essential. Someone should inspect the entire propulsion system annually. A clean bill of health means that the fuel tank has been checked for water, the V-belts have been inspected for wear, and several dozen other potential Achilles' heels have been looked at. A knowledgeable owner may be able to assume such responsibilities; if not, finding a yard with these competencies is essential. Hiring a yard mechanic to go along on a spring launching sea trial can be a good investment.

Specialization can be an important factor. Many yards focus on a specific type of powerboat. Some facilities work predominantly on the high-performance boats; others service the family cruiser segment of the market. By being able to specialize, a facility can fine-tune certain skills, and the boat owner benefits from the detailed experience a mechanic gains on other jobs. If a craftsman

Stack storage of powerboats is growing in popularity all over the United States.

Fork lifts are the workhorses of stack storage operations.

Performance boats normally require more attention than family runabouts. If possible, look for a yard that specializes in your type of craft.

has seen 10 other cases of the same problem your vessel is suffering from, the chances are good that he will be able to make a cost-effective diagnosis and repair.

Many of the major engine manufacturers supplying the powerboat market run extensive training programs and certification systems. This link between the factory and the boatyard/marina service center is a valuable asset, and it's worth inquiring whether or not the yard's mechanics are factory trained. Many operations proudly frame certificates and mount them in their shops. Remember, however, that a piece of paper doesn't necessarily guarantee good work; it's just another factor in the mosaic that communicates a yard's reputation. Regardless of how neat the shop is, how well-schooled the mechanics are, and how complete the tool inventory seems to be, employee attitude is the crucial element.

3

Economics of the Modern Boatyard

S OMETIMES A YARD CLIENT may wonder where his boatyard owner is salting away the fortunes that he's making. The client looks at his yard bills, counts the number of boats in the yard, and visualizes checks being wired in the spring and fall to Switzerland or the Cayman Islands. As a yard manager, I can only respond, "Would that it were so!"

At a recent meeting of the American Boat Builders and Repairers Association (ABBRA), members of a panel comprising boat owners, the yachting press, and a marine surveyor were invited to comment on the industry. Predictably, the first salvo fired was about the high cost of boat maintenance. In response, yard owner and former ABBRA president Tom Hale pointed out that a boatyard, like many small businesses, is a mirror reflecting local economic conditions. Labor rates seen in auto repair bills, plumbers' and electricians' statements, and general contracting costs also influence what goes on in boatyards. Unlike other small businesses, however, most boatyards have little choice about operating in the high-rent district. With waterfront property leading the real estate spiral, land value and the resulting tax structure have had a dramatic effect upon overhead. Add to this significant increases in insurance premiums, escalating energy costs, and ever-growing expenses for materials, and one gets some idea of why boatyard rates continue to climb.

To stay afloat in today's competitive business world, many boatyards are becoming marine marketing centers. (Bend Boat Basin, Portsmouth, Rhode Island)

Crane storage puts boats about three feet apart in long aisles. The more valuable the property, the greater the dense-packing.

Boatyards, like other small businesses, benefit from sound economic decision making. Yard owners and administrators closely monitor profit and loss statistics, which portray the dynamics of their operation. As a boating consumer, you should be aware of the basic financial structure of boatyards. It will help you to better understand the services they offer, and also the constraints under which they operate. Good craftsmanship and good management don't always go hand in hand, but successful operations tend to have a grip on the business aspects, as well as the workmanship factors, involved in the industry.

HOW DOES A BOATYARD MAKE MONEY?

Let's imagine that a boatyard owner decides to hire three additional mechanics and spend the winter rebuilding diesel engines. We'll assume that these efforts generate $50,000 of additional income. The added revenue seems to indicate that the effort might be a financially productive one. But a good manager will not make such an assumption until he has carefully established the costs involved on a per-dollar-billed basis.

When a boatyard owner I know actually tried this scheme, the results were discouraging. As with any labor-intensive endeavor, salary was the biggest expense factor. Of each dollar earned in the diesel rebuilds, 72% went to employee wages; 26% could be attributed to parts and supplies; 2% was left to cover the overhead (insurance, heat, light, and taxes). Profit? Forget it. What had been assumed to be a revenue maker was clearly a loss. A close analysis of the numbers revealed that the amount of labor needed to rebuild each engine was about twice what had been anticipated. Problems with broken bolts, modified components, and other unexpected delays kept the time clock running. If the yard had passed the full cost of this labor on to the owner, a rebuild would have cost significantly more than a new engine.

At first, the manager assumed the staff had been incompetent or inaccurate with the time figures. He and the mechanical foreman went through the process step-by-step and discovered

Engine rebuilds are labor intensive and rarely cost effective.

Many yards combine sales and service operations.

what most yards have reluctantly accepted; today's labor rates make in-house engine rebuilding a poor revenue producer. Some small engine shops and freelance mechanics can offer cost-effective rebuilds, due to their specialization and lower overhead, but most successful yards have switched their focus from a mechanical rebuilding facility to sales, service, and installation of new engines—an example of keeping pace with a changing economy.

The day of inexpensive waterfront property and seasonal work is drawing to a close. For today's yard to succeed financially, it must be able to do volume business and be multifaceted when it comes to generating revenues. The most profitable operations seem to be a bit of a three-ring circus. They sell repair labor, build boats, accrue storage revenue, offer mooring and slip options, and rent space for or operate their own chandleries, brokerage businesses, restaurants, sail lofts, electronics dealerships, etc. Yards are becoming marine marketing centers, or they are closing up and being turned into condominium sites.

Pressures of Property Values

Alternate land use is affecting boatyard operations in much the same way it has affected farmers. Real estate moguls look for highly desirable waterfront property. They seek out businesses that earn a small portion of what high-density housing would yield. Shoreside condominiums and town houses have a proven track record, and big dollar speculators are ready to hand yard owners fat checks for the deeds to their land. Such one-time, big killings have been enough incentive for many yard owners to turn over the keys to the travelift. This practice has grown so detrimental to boaters that in some areas, such as Marblehead, Massachusetts, local government has enacted zoning code changes, which mandate that specific sites remain boatyards.

The law of supply and demand enters into the picture. In areas where yards are being turned into trendy waterfront housing, boat owners are faced with a nautical version of musical chairs. Too few yards and too many boats fuel the fire of rising costs.

Rescue boat launching ramp: the only open waterfront in Marblehead, Massachusetts. Skyrocketing property values have put many boatyards out of business.

Waterfront docks and condominiums opposite historic Mystic, Connecticut.

Storage charges increase, and boat owners look to other options, such as golf.

Overhead

Overhead is a crucial concern to every boatyard. The fellow with a van and a box of tools may charge a customer $25 an hour for his services. The nearby yard charges $35 an hour for the same work. The yard must pay taxes and maintain buildings and equipment, docks, floats, and piers. In addition, there is insurance, holiday pay, retirement plans, and other worker benefits. Capital expenditures can run to five and six digits and well beyond. A 35-ton travelift may cost $84,000; the pier it runs on an additional $60,000. New hydraulic cranes cost more than two Porsches. Slip construction, docks, and shop facilities are all significant capital outlays. The operator must recoup these costs and the interest the bank happily charges. Most yard administrators recognize that in order to meet their overhead, they need to bill a customer at a rate of about three times what the craftsman's wage actually is. This may seem exorbitant, but it is actually similar to other small, service-oriented businesses.

Labor Costs

It is not easy to find skilled, productive employees. Many boatyard operations prefer to hire untrained individuals with good character traits, then utilize in-house training to develop the individual's skills. Although this is seldom a formal educational approach, it does seem to work, and has become an Americanized version of the formal European apprentice system. Unfortunately, this process has been jeopardized by pricing discrepancies among industries. Time and time again employees who have been trained in a good boatyard find that far more money and benefits are available in other fields. The price structure of the marine industry prevents it from competing with other, more profitable ventures. Consequently, many skilled and productive craftsmen move on to other trades.

In my survey of boatyards, labor rates ranged from $22 an hour to $48 an hour. The median was $35 an hour and most yards seemed to cluster within a few dollars of this amount. Geographic location does not seem to have as much impact on labor rates as it has in the past. Some say that this has something to do with how far afield the New York Yacht Club Summer Cruise has been venturing. But the fact is travelifts cost about the same in every state, and, although labor costs do vary a bit, it isn't enough to offset the other expenses of doing business.

There's no denying that labor rates have had a significant impact on some of the activities traditionally associated with boatyards. Some operations still build boats. Today's economy, however, tends to hinder such efforts. For example, a custom 45-foot sloop may require 10,000 hours to build. If the yard labor rate is $35 an hour, a mind-boggling $350,000 figure results. This should be added to the cost of materials and expensive equipment that go into the construction of a fine yacht. Most builders discount their new construction labor. They realize that building keeps their skilled craftsmen on the job, but the bottom-line financial figures

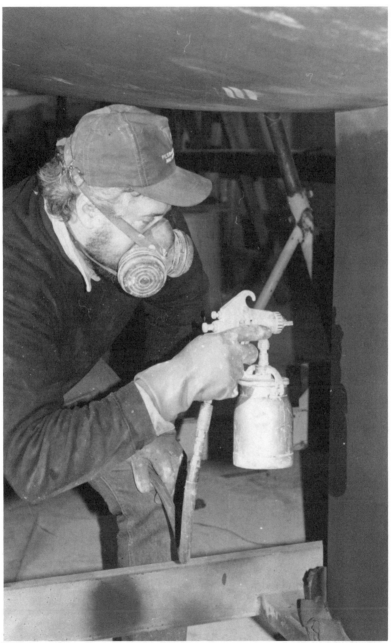

Skilled professionals are the backbone of a yard's reputation—and its major operating expense.

Topside repairs are a major sale item in many repair yards.

Putting the finishing touches on George Coumanteros's SORC racer Boomerang *at the Derecktor Shipyard in Mamaroneck, New York. Although boatbuilding is rarely profitable, skilled craftsmanship enormously enhances a yard's reputation.*

remind them that repair and refit work, billed at a nondiscounted labor rate, are far more profitable. Those yards that continue to be involved in boatbuilding do so primarily because of its skill-building nature, and its value to a yard's reputation. These operations accept the fact that the profit margin is not what repair work may provide. But by scheduling their building efforts to coincide with slack time in the repair business, they tend not to sacrifice much cost effectiveness. The on-the-job training this offers their employees certainly enhances craftsmanship. A similar case could be made for the yard that initially loses money on engine rebuilds. It may also benefit in the long run. In situations where the work done is good, such mechanical endeavors may act as an advertisement, generating a significant increase in repair business.

The opposite is also true; bad news travels fast. The experienced yard administrator realizes that word-of-mouth and waterfront gossip are one of the most important communication factors in the industry.

Impact of Insurance Costs

Insurance issues are one of the more serious concerns facing today's boatyard and marina owners. In our litigious society, the waterfront can be a hazardous surrounding. Horror stories abound, detailing personal injury situations where courts find marine facilities at fault. Add to this the cost of fire, theft, and damage loss insurance, and it's not hard to understand why many owners cringe at the thought of insurance premiums.

Court settlements have bankrupted more than a few boat-yards. Today lawyers utilize a shotgun approach, suing everyone even remotely involved with an incident hinting of negligence. In boating related accidents, it's not unusual to hear of a yard, uninvolved with an injury, being brought into a lawsuit because of work done at the yard years before. Insurance companies closely

Fences, gatehouses, and warning signs are a growing part of the boatyard environment in today's litigious society.

Firefighting equipment is insurance-mandated at many yards.

Inside storage at Yacht Haven West (Stamford, Connecticut). Although per-foot storage fees are higher than for outside storage, they are offset by reduced maintenance costs and in some cases reduced insurance premiums.

monitor the precedents set in such situations and amend their coverage and premium rates accordingly.

The yard owner looking into insurance needs quickly discovers that there are various types of coverage available. Some insure low-risk activities and involve modest premiums, while others are identified as high-risk issues and carry a staggering premium. Most insurance companies perform a risk evaluation survey in which the marina or boatyard is closely scrutinized. High-risk activities and dangerous structures are noted. Past insurance records are reviewed. Items such as indoor storage, covered slips, presence or absence of a do-it-yourself policy, and building code wiring violations are carefully noted. Once a profile of a tentative client's business is assembled, risk statistics can be calculated. Those operations doing a large volume of what is considered "hazardous work" may be deemed a poor risk. Their premiums will be high; in some cases, they may even be refused coverage.

Most yards purchase coverage against damage, bodily injury, fire, theft, and liability. Some also tie in employee medical/dental, and life insurance programs. It's easy to see how insurance premiums can evolve into a significant expenditure.

BOATYARD COMPARISON SHOPPING

The foregoing discussion, combined with our earlier discussion about the relationship between quality and cost effectiveness, should help the boat owner to better appreciate the factors involved in boatyard pricing structures and the potential pitfalls of comparison shopping based solely on cost analysis. Finding the right boatyard is a compromise between quality, range of services available, location, labor rates, and do-it-yourself options. A variety of packages are available; some of the more typical ones are discussed below.

Boat owners who do their homework seem to have the least

Most yards bill mast storage and handling separately.

What to do with cradles during the sailing season? Some yards assess a summer storage fee.

amount of trouble. This includes thoroughly going over the literature that a yard puts out listing the services it offers. Don't skip to the price per foot statistics and ignore the rest. Carefully read the description of what each charge includes. All too often what is part of a fixed price in one yard will be an extra cost at another. A written comparison of several different options provides a good starting point for an evaluation.

Those who wish to compare several winter storage options must be ready to interpret a variety of billing methods. Some facilities charge by the square foot while others base their rates on a LOA (length overall) measurement. Most yards treat mast handling and storage as a separate item. Some bill by the length of the spar times a fixed rate, while others operate on a labor rate basis. You will probably notice that in some yards the HSL (hauling/storing/launching) fee covers everything from unstepping and stepping to a quick prep and a coat of bottom paint in the spring. Other yards follow an à la carte approach with separate charges for each item. The best way to get a feel for what these numbers mean is to do some calculations and compare identical work orders extended under each pricing system. What looks to be the most expensive option on a per-foot basis may turn out to be the best buy after all.

Labor rates can be deceiving. For instance, some craftsmen work faster than others and deliver the same quality. More work accomplished in less time can significantly offset a higher hourly rate. There are also variations among yards with regard to policies toward when the meter actually starts running. In some facilities the time clock starts ticking as soon as an employee punches the job card; other operations bill only for the time actually involved in the task at hand. Differences such as these can quickly erode an apparent bargain.

While we're on the subject of bargains, those who enjoy such hands-on endeavors as well as those who wish to save on maintenance costs should pay heed to the yard's maintenance policies. It's important to find out exactly what do-it-yourself stipulations exist. Many operations insist that all bottom work be done by the yard staff. Fewer and fewer yards allow full freedom to owners hoping to cope with their own maintenance needs. If the bottom line dollar-and-cents calculations are your primary motivation, it may make sense to pay a slightly higher hauling/storing/launching fee at a "do-it yourself" yard rather than opt for a minor HSL savings and the significantly greater cost of professional maintenance.

To make sure that apples are being compared with apples, the cost-conscious boat owner needs firm data upon which to base decisions. Tactfully clarify the following details with the yard manager:

- Does the yard give estimates?
- Are they fixed?
- If not, how flexible are they?
- Are more repetitive tasks flat-rated?
- Is there a published price list?
- What is included in the hauling/storage/launching price?

- How are mast storage, bottom cleaning, and jack stand rentals handled?
- What is the yard policy toward do-it-yourself work?
- Must supplies and materials be purchased at the yard's store?
- Are water and electricity readily available?

The following chart represents a sample comparison shopping guide for five boatyards. The yards listed are hypothetical, although actual examples of each type of operation exit in abundance. (For a description of several quality operations, see Appendix.) The chart establishes several categories of services and evaluates them on a scale of 1 to 5 (1 is poor; 5 is excellent). In addition, costs and special considerations are listed, along with a brief commentary below. The results are enlightening:

Faraway Yacht Haven: Cost-conscious boat owners with a strong wanderlust will probably carefully explore the possibility of hauling out at Faraway Yacht Haven The cost of storage is about half what local yards charge. The workmanship is good, and the labor rate appears to be a bargain. Unfortunately, distance can be an expensive variable. Those facing a major refit may find it cost effective to choose such an option; otherwise, the distance factor usually negates any potential savings.

Royal Yachts, Ltd: Those for whom cost is no obstacle choose this boatyard hands down. Quality workmanship prevails, with a price tag to match. An experienced management team recommends refit needs, and a computer tracks the history of each vessel and compiles custom-tailored preventive maintenance recommendations. Boat owners spend more than twice what the average outlay is at other yards, but their vessels look better, are more maintenance-free during the boating season, and sustain fewer breakdowns. This type of complete custodial service is a great option for those who can afford it.

Local Marine: This small, family operation consists of a father and son team, who personally care for about 75 sailboats and powerboats in the 25-foot to 45-foot range. The father is a veteran mechanic, with an uncanny ability to find simple, effective solutions to engine problems. His son is a skilled craftsman who does good work and does it noticeably faster than the competition. Local Marine is usually over-subscribed, but the family does not want to expand; their goals revolve around fine-tuning the existing operation. Boat owners who recognize cost-effective quality are willing to wait in line.

Bargain Boatyard: At this yard one pays less and gets less. The equipment is old and poorly maintained, and the services are minimal and often of dubious quality. Those who use the yard tend to be of two mindsets. The first is a group of competent do-it-yourselfers who need inexpensive haulouts and storage. The second group is composed of those seeking more for less and, at least initially, not realizing that what they have found is less for less. A sizable annual turnover seems to indicate that it takes only one season to clarify the picture. Poor quality workmanship is a bitter pill at any cost.

Ocean Marine: This yard represents a good compromise between the gold-plater service of Royal Yachts, Ltd. and the minimalism of Bargain Boatyard. Workmanship is good, with the possible exception of carpentry skills. The equipment is carefully maintained, and the yard is a clean, well-organized operation, whose management and employees go out of their way to meet the needs of their clients. Pricing is straightforward and solidly mid-range; it buys quality service delivered on time. Ocean Marine is a good example of a "you get what you pay for" yard.

Yards are as unique as the clients they serve. The one you choose must meet your own specific requirements. Once you can define these, you have made the most important step toward picking a yard that is cost effective for you.

BOATYARD EVALUATION SURVEY
COMPARATIVE COSTS FOR A 30-FOOT SLOOP

Boatyard Name	Faraway Yacht Haven Migratory Bay		Royal Yachts, Ltd. Upper Cove	
Workmanship quality (1=poor; 5=tops)	mechanical paint fiberglass	4 5 3	mechanical paint rig	5 5 5
Hauling equipment and condition (1=poor; 5=tops)	railway to 30 tons elevator lift to 150 tons	3 4 4	travelift: 35-, 50-, and 150-ton	5
Attitude of personnel (1=poor; 5=tops)	manager staff	4 4	manager staff	5 5
Labor Rates/Hour	general skilled	$20 $24	general electrical mechanical paint	$40 $45 $45 $45
Work Order Estimates (See Note 1)	$450 plus materials		$1,250 plus materials	
Storage costs	$18/ft HSL (includes unstep/ step and cradle. Pressure spray $35)		$35/ft HSL (includes unstep/ step, pressure spray, jack stand rental)	
Scaled cost for Winter HSL (See Note 2)	$540.00 35.00 $575.00		$1,050.00	
Do-It-Yourself Limitations	no limits		no exterior work; no subcontract	
Projected Total Less Materials	$ 450.00 575.00 $1,025.00		$1,250.00 1,050.00 $2,300.00	
Special Considerations	yard 1,200 miles away in Canada		large, first class facility; $300 minimum at yard chandlery	

Note 1   Bottom prep and paint; engine winterization and commissioning; topsides
clean and wax.

BOATYARD EVALUATION SURVEY
COMPARATIVE COSTS FOR A 30-FOOT SLOOP

Local Marine Nearby Harbor		Bargain Boatyard Mud Creek		Ocean Marine Nearby Harbor	
mechanical	5	mechanical	1	mechanical	3–4
paint	3	paint	2	paint	4
				carpentry	2
travelift: 15-ton	4	crane: 20-ton p&h with spreader bar	2–3	travelift: 20- and 50-ton	4
manager	5	manager	2	manager	4
staff	3	staff	2	staff	3–4
all	$28	general	$26	general	$20
		skilled	$28	rig	$32
				mechanical	$36
				paint	$33
$675 plus materials		$525 plus materials		$650 plus materials	
$27/ft HSL (includes unstep/ step & cleaning. Mast storage $270; jack stands $10/stand)		$22/ft HSL (unstep/step. Mast storage $260; cradle rental $50; pressure spray $1/ft.)		$26/ft HSL (unstep/step: time and materials. Jack stands $15/stand; pressure spray $50)	
$ 810.00 270.00 50.00 $1,130.00		$ 660.00 260.00 50.00 30.00 $1,000.00		$ 780.00 320.00 75.00 50.00 $1,225.00	
bottom must be yard done		no limits		no work below rail done by owner	
$1,130.00 675.00 $1,805.00		$ 525 1,000 $1,525.00		$1,225.00 650.00 $1,875.00	
small operation; manager also yard mechanic; top- quality repair work		run down equipment		organized yard; excellent appearance	

Note 2   Includes basic HSL; unstep, store, and step mast; jack stand or cradle rental;
pressure spray.

4

Marinas

M ARINAS, SOME SAY, ARE as much a natural part of
boating as a manicured lawn is part of a forest. True, they
are mandatory where room for moorings is limited. But in too
many cases they tend to turn boats into cottages and keep sailors in
ports. Those who take a traditional attitude toward the subject insist
that boats belong on moorings; as slips proliferate, seamanship
declines.

Whether there is truth to these assertions or merely prejudice,
the fact remains that marinas are here to stay. For the past 50 years
they have slowly evolved, and today's gradual change, steady
growth, and increasing rates depict a mature industry. On the East
Coast there is only a 10% annual turnover among marina
residents—due mainly to individuals entering and leaving boating.
The West Coast sees about a 30% turnover, although it's hard to get
accurate data from areas like Marina del Ray, where the black
market slip business may be larger than the actual upfront version.

The reason for this steady growth of marinas is in large part
economic—it is yet another reflection of the escalating pressure on
waterfront property. In fact, in the past few years the concept of
marina ownership has been rethought and a new growth industry
has evolved: slip ownership and long-term leasing. For the
conventional boatyard or marina operation, the cash generated
from such a sale or lease provides equity for capital improvements;
the boat owner, meanwhile, is better protected from economic

Goat Island Marina, Newport, Rhode Island.

fluctuation and changes in waterfront land usage that threaten many boatyards and marinas. There has also been a significant interest among speculators, who see this trend as a ripe opportunity for a quick round of hefty profits.

The floating futures market has caught on. Sailors on both coasts like the continuity offered by a long-term lease—usually 99 years. Entrepreneurs like the opportunity for lucrative short-term investments. According to Ed Doherty, from Marina Consult, of Cataumet, Massachusetts, condo-slips and long-term leases are the waterfront wave of the future. He cites one situation in Cape Cod where slips were initially selling at $33,000; two years later they were selling at $130,000. At Ocean Reef, Florida, slips that initially sold for $60,000 to $70,000 were in 1987 approaching $250,000. Speculators realize the finite nature of waterfront access. Only time will tell whether the practice of charging what the market will bear will turn slip sitting into a true Vanderbilt tradition.

Purists may feel that marinas are peripheral to boating while

Boatyard/marina combinations are an example of effective land utilization and make good economic sense in today's high-rent waterfront districts. (Bend Boat Basin)

Bulkheads, piers, and floating docks: the heart of a dredged yacht basin.

boatyards are essential, but a combined operation makes good economic sense. Boatyards and marinas are as natural a combination as a filling station and automotive service center; after all, boats need attention both in season and out of season. A waterfront facility capable of meeting these needs is an example of effective land utilization, and large and small dual-focus facilities are thriving all over the world. Many feel that waterfront land is too expensive not to consider using its full potential.

Choosing the right marina involves a lot more than simply finding a float to tie up to. Influencing factors range from safety and social concerns to the ever-present financial constraints. Whether it's a short stay at the Quay in Papeete, Tahiti, or a more permanent residence behind Santa Barbara's stone seawall, be sure you understand what's involved in safe, cost-effective marina berthing.

LOCATION

Begin your quest for a marina with a general overview. Determine how major physical factors such as wind, tide, and swell conditions influence the water surrounding your boat's prospective new home. Weather patterns vary in different parts of the world, and so do the requirements for safe shelter. Just as there are differences between a safe fair-weather anchorage and a hurricane hole, there are variations in marina protection. In regions of the country where the boating season coincides with tranquil weather and calm seas, docks and slips are often built in rather exposed locations. These may be fine for an evening layover, but they are probably not a good choice for those who may want to leave their boats for several weeks at a time.

It's important to look closely at the geometry of the basin. How are the slips located in reference to the prevailing wind direction? From which quadrant do gale force winds normally arrive? Pay particular attention to fetch. Fetch is an oceanographer's term that refers to the distance over which wind from a specific direction can affect the water on which it is blowing. For example, if a marina is situated at the northern end of a 12-mile-long lake, it will be exposed to a 12-mile fetch when the winds are southerly. A bay or lake that appears as tranquil as a pond can change into a seething cauldron whenever the wind howls across open water. Marinas exposed to long fetches need breakwaters or wave baffles to tame the swells that develop.

Many west coast marinas are directly affected by ocean swells. Fortunately—in most cases—the Army Corps of Engineers has built substantial jetties and breakwaters in an effort to control the problems. But even though waves are kept out of the marina basins, many basins experience strong surging during heavy weather. This rhythmic undulation of the water in the harbor tends to chafe docklines at an alarming rate. Good anti-chafe gear and doubled-up docklines are a must. The larger swells of the winter months tend to move sand in what oceanographers refer to as the littoral current. This downcoast conveyor of sediment has been interrupted by the Corps of Engineers' endeavors. Sand is now often deposited in excess at the upcoast jetties and eroded away from those on the downcoast side. Many marina entrances must be continually dredged in order to keep them open for navigation. Large swells, born in the winter storms of the Aleutian Gulf, have been known to close off harbor entrances in Southern California and Hawaii. Are the jetties at the entrance to your marina an attraction to large swells or protection against them? The local surfers know the answer.

Safety must be a primary concern for those who are slip shopping. Unfortunately it isn't always easy to determine where dangers might exist. It's hard to forget how pleased the boat owners of Ventura, California were with their new marina and low slip fees. Very few took note of the fact that the Corps of Engineers had chosen to build the harbor adjacent to the Santa Clara, a "usually dry river bed." But then a particularly vicious winter storm changed the character of the river—and the fortunes of the marina. In the middle of a black squally night the no-longer-dormant Santa Clara rose over its leveed banks and flooded into the marina with the force of a tidal wave. Boats, docks, and piers were flushed into the ocean, where huge seas drove them back onto the shore. In the morning the sun broke through the clouds and revealed an eerie sight. The shore was a giant collage of docks, boats, and debris. Some vessels were pulverized on the beach, yet still tied to their portion of a marina float. One sloop lay on its side with rig intact, and hardly a smudge on its starboard topside, but on the port side there were holes large enough to walk through. The devastation was awesome. Horror stories such as these serve as a reminder that it's hard to be too cautious when evaluating safety parameters. Use not only your eyes, but your imagination.

SAFE ENGINEERING

Be sure the pilings that hold the float you may be tying your boat to are long enough to accommodate the rise of a storm tide. All too often the tide goes unnoticed. Marina builders allow for its normal range, including bimonthly spring tides, but not enough consideration is given to the atypical effect of a really severe storm. When barometric pressure drops, the water level rises. Add to this the effect of a storm surge, which causes water to pile up ahead of gusting winds, and the result can be tides as much as 10 feet above

If the tidal range is minimal, floating docks are unnecessary.

normal. Short pilings and piers may be awash, while floats and boats become free agents. Loss of support structures at the peak of a storm can spell disaster.

Dock and float construction is another important consideration. Wood, steel, aluminum, reinforced plastics, and concrete all are in use, and as with boatbuilding, there are good and bad versions of each. The most common dangers arise from basic shortcomings. Take, for example, a solidly built pier surrounded by well-designed and constructed floating docks. The entire structure can be threatened by inadequate pilings. Poles that have been hydro-jetted (set by high pressure water drilling), and not driven to refusal, may not be able to support the loads imposed by the docks and floats. In many areas, untreated, non-creosoted pilings are subject to rapid deterioration from marine organisms. An inadequate number of pilings can't provide the support needed, no matter how carefully driven and treated.

Building scantlings that are more than adequate in one

Tall pilings and well-made floating docks suggest quality construction.

location may be grossly inadequate in another. Seasonal changes in weather patterns can make a big difference. Many marinas in the Northeast were designed for summer use only. Some have now been converted to year-round, in-the-water storage facilities, with bubble systems to keep the ice problem at bay. However, more volatile weather patterns can reveal serious structural inadequacies. In situations where there is no breakwater to intercept seas generated by violent winter gales, extensive damage to boats and docks can result. The more severe the winter weather pattern is, the more bullet-proof a marina's protection should be.

There is a big difference between tying alongside a fixed pier and next to a floating dock. The former can be a real problem in areas where there are strong winds and large tidal ranges. Fender boards and springlines need to be regularly inspected and replaced. Floating docks rise and fall with the tide, allowing for better use of fenders and lines. While they are usually more convenient, they are a more costly option as well.

While you're visiting a potential new home for your boat, take a look at the availability of water and electricity. These are nice amenities that are available in most marinas. But beware of questionable looking power hook-ups. Water and electricity can be a dangerous combination, and electrical deficiencies have been known to cause fires, hazardous shocks, and electrolysis. State and local building codes require certain safety factors, but ask the dockmaster if there is a ground fault interrupt system (it should protect every outlet in the marina). Ask also if isolation transformers are recommended. Many boaters like the way these devices separate the shore wiring from that of the boats.

MOORINGS AND LAUNCH SERVICE

Many marinas keep a majority of their clients on well-maintained moorings and provide regular launch service, particularly in areas where exposure to certain wind and sea directions presents a danger to floating slips. One of the biggest potential problems with such arrangements is spacing. The tighter the pattern, the more boats can be packed into a given area. But correct placement of boats in a fleet requires more than a grid pattern mentality. The individual characteristics of each vessel and variables such as wind, tide, and current must be taken into account. Shortcuts can be dangerous.

Swinging room is a critical issue. Each vessel needs enough distance from other boats to compensate for the scope of the ground tackle it is tethered to. When measuring out spacing requirements it must be understood that the current, as well as the shape and the drift characteristics of a vessel, can cause one boat to move in one direction while its neighbor heads the other way. For example, a deep draft sailboat with low freeboard might stream in the direction of the current while an adjacent high-sided powerboat is following the wind direction. Wind against tide situations can cause collisions in a poorly planned mooring area.

No boat ever broke free because its mooring equipment was excessively strong. Hard and fast data regarding the relationship between boat size and mooring anchor poundage vary according to bottom composition and exposure to wind and sea conditions. In some well-protected bays, 40-foot sloops lie contentedly on 250-pound mushroom anchors. In exposed, hard-bottom areas, a similar sized vessel may be able to drag a 500-pound mushroom anchor all over the bay. A boat owner's best option is to see what the professionals recommend for the specific local conditions and make sure the moorings your marina sets out are at least that size—and preferably one size larger.

Marinas using moorings for some or all of their customers need to maintain reliable launch service. Most operations seem to opt for diesel-powered launches between 18 and 30 feet long. A good launch must have agile handling characteristics, and, since it will be approaching vessels from the starboard side, its drivetrain should end with a right-hand rotating propeller. This allows the operator to move the stern to port (bringing the launch parallel to the larger boat) by briefly throttling up immediately after shifting into reverse. It also enables him or her to move away from the vessel in forward gear with the stern tending to stay well to starboard and therefore away from the shiny topside of the yacht where the stop has just been made.

Ketch Arabella *moored in usually tranquil Oyster Bay, New York.*

Not-so-tranquil Oyster Bay in the grip of Hurricane Gloria, September 1985. Be sure the mooring gear your marina provides is strong enough to stand up to a blow.

FACILITIES

Many marinas provide showers, laundry facilities, and marine chandleries. Some provide tennis courts and swimming pools, and some are associated with an adjacent yacht club. Keep in mind that clubs vary in format and outlook. In some areas tradition reigns, and neckties, yachting caps, and blue blazers are essential sporting attire. In other areas formal clubhouse dining mandates only shoes and a T-shirt. At first these issues may seem insignificant, but don't underestimate them. A dockside marina is like any other community. Those who have more in common with the flock seem to find additional social satisfaction.

Look over dockside social dynamics as carefully as you inspect the physical structure of the facility. Take notice of who the residents are and what they do with their boats. Sailors and powerboaters often seek different experiences from the sea. The same holds true for the time they spend at the dock. Be sure you feel at home with your potential neighbors. Spend some time discussing the marina with them. Usually you'll hear about what works and what doesn't; who parties all night; and who to watch out for as he heads toward a downwind slip. It's nice to get a feeling for the neighborhood before you move in.

A marina can be the starting point of many lasting friendships. It's hard to forget the year my family and I spent on D dock in Channel Islands Harbor Marina, California. We were fitting out *Wind Shadow* for a world cruise, and so were a few of our neighbors. Together we speculated about what landfalls in Rarotonga and Raeatea would be like. We fitted self-steering vanes to the transoms of our boats and tinkered our way to eventual readiness. Common interests turned a collection of floating docks into a very human experience.

It's sad to say, but security is also a vital concern. Fences, locks, and gate keepers are not a solution, just a response to a growing problem. If possible, choose safe alternatives, rather than relying on alarm systems and barriers. Peace of mind about your boat is worth a few extra dollars and miles driven. Don't underestimate the

Ice and fuel are essential commodities at most marinas.

Chandleries, restaurants, and boutiques are among the facilities offered at many full-service marinas. (Dauntless, Essex, Connecticut)

A marina is a community as well as a place to tie alongside, and those who have more in common with the flock tend to find additional boating satisfaction. This Bahamian marina caters to large powerboats and sport fishermen.

Typical marina on the Intracoastal Waterway. For cruising sailors, marina layovers can be the starting point of lasting friendships.

drawback of keeping your vessel in a marina that is well protected from the sea, but is wide open to an active population of thieves.

While we're on the subject of security, look closely at your boat owner's insurance policy. Be sure that your coverage includes protection for what might go wrong in your marina slip or mooring area. For example, suppose you have long-term leased or purchased your slip and during a particularly nasty storm your boat is heavily damaged and the floating slip breaks free. Most policies cover repairs or even replacement of the vessel due to such an act of God. But what happens if your floating dock seriously damages a half dozen other boats in the process? Who is accountable for this situation? Don't merely assume that the marina is. Marina and boatyard insurance coverage focuses mainly on protecting these operations from expensive out-of-pocket legal settlements. It is not meant to be a cushion for the boat owner. He or she is expected to and in many cases required to have certain insurance coverage. Be sure that you have discussed your needs with a broker familiar with the marine insurance market.

COMPARISON SHOPPING

The cost of marina berthing can vary from almost reasonable to outrageous depending on the part of the world you live in and the kinds of amenities you require. The cost of tying up alongside is nearly always significantly more than that of tying up to a mooring and rowing ashore.

As in any decision, there are important trade-offs involved in finding the right marina. To help you evaluate which option is best for you, I have included the following marina evaluation form, summarizing some of the major criteria to be taken into consideration when comparison shopping for a marina that fits both your boating style and your pocketbook.

MARINA EVALUATION FORM

Marina _____

Address _____

PROTECTION FROM WIND/SEA/CURRENT

CONSTRUCTION QUALITY OF DOCKS/FLOATS

APPROPRIATENESS OF SLIP/MOORING AVAILABLE

SOCIAL ATMOSPHERE

SECURITY CONCERNS

SHORESIDE FACILITIES

AESTHETIC ISSUES

OTHER ISSUES

COST

5

Cost-Saving Alternatives

T HERE'S NO DOUBT THAT quality service at a traditional boatyard is expensive. When it comes to haulouts and winter storage, frugal owners look toward dollar-saving alternatives to the conventional boatyard. Particularly if the owner is a willing and reasonably competent do-it-yourselfer, these can work out well. They can also lead to disaster. The intent of this chapter is to lay out guidelines for those seeking to spend as little as possible and still reasonably care for their vessels.

Mobility can play a vital role. Some owners avoid costly winter layups by sailing to warmer climates. Others combine cruising plans with refits in less costly parts of the country—or world, for that matter. I personally recall the splendid sailing and bountiful harbors of New Zealand's northeast coast. That nation also has an abundance of fine yards offering a full range of marine services. In such areas, superior service is marketed at very modest prices. Canadian refits might also offer an attractive option for U.S. sailors.

If an owner knows what to look for, a foreign refit may be both a bargain and a unique cultural experience. But the attractiveness of this option can vary considerably from situation to situation. Sometimes quality suffers. In other situations the surroundings leave much to be desired. Most important, there are no dependable shortcuts to locating and arranging such a refit. Although foreign yards occasionally advertise in American boating magazines, it is difficult to judge the quality of an operation from a distance. The

For those free to wander, traveling south for the winter can be a way to beat the high storage costs found in the Northeast—and save on refits as well.

only reliable way is actually to travel to the country under consideration (either on a cruise or by land) and go through the same evaluation procedure described earlier in this book. It is strongly advised that the boat owner, the banker he is dealing with, and the yard manager all be fluent in the same language.

The same alternate vendor concept can be pursued on a regional basis. Those tired of the high labor rates and storage costs found in the Northeast may find better bargains in the Carolinas and Georgia. Many parts of Florida abound with yards that will stretch the refit dollar. For years, big boat sailors from New England have been sailing their boats south, in early autumn, for protected waters of the Chesapeake Bay. They are able to extend their cruising season by a few weeks and also avail themselves of less costly, top-quality boatyards. Those contemplating a bit of wandering under sail and who are interested in stretching their boating budgets should give serious thought to regional refit advantages.

Wet Storage

Many of those unable to sail south for the winter consider wet storage. Marinas have adopted bubbler systems, submerged turbine-like fans, and other ingenious methods to circulate warmer bottom water upwards, preventing ice from forming around boats, docks, floats, etc. The past few mild winters have convinced many owners that this must be the way to go. The cost for such storage is usually 50 to 65% of what dry storage runs. If the slips are well protected from winter gales, and the marina security is dependable, it can be a viable alternative. Keep in mind, however, that your boat is afloat, and though small, there is a certain degree of risk involved. I recall the tale of a friend who nearly lost a very fine 48-foot wooden yawl. Maintained to quality yacht standards, she was annually wet-stored in a yard on the Eastern Shore of the Chesapeake. Halfway through the winter, her owner was informed that his pride and joy had nearly sunk in the slip. The engine and reverse gear had been submerged. A close inspection revealed that a small electric pump, used to circulate raw water to cool the refrigeration condenser, had been the source of the leak. It had been plumbed into a cockpit drain through-hull whose seacock had been left open to accommodate heavy rain. The pump design required that it be placed at a point below the waterline. A cold snap caused the air in the bilge to drop below freezing, and the water in the plastic pump body froze and cracked the housing. When the temperature rose, a leak resulted that nearly sank the soundly constructed yawl.

I've seen boats built with rigid PVC pipe used for cockpit drain plumbing. Extending this below the waterline is a gamble in any climate. In frigid winter weather, it is an invitation for serious problems. Those who choose wet storage as their winter option must keep in mind that no boat yard or marina I know of offers a flotation guarantee.

Leaving the Mast Stepped

Many sailors are choosing to store their boats with the masts stepped, thereby avoiding hundreds of dollars of costs involved in

Winter wet storage, here assisted by a bubbler system, involves a degree of risk but can result in substantial savings.

Well-covered, wet-stored boats. But some provision needs to be made for ventilation.

Leaving the mast stepped can significantly reduce your yard bill. But be sure your boat's blocking system is adequate for the additional weight and windage aloft.

unstepping. Indeed, there is usually no need to remove a modern, properly rigged mast each year. As with many shortcuts, though, there are side effects to be considered. The increased windage and leverage imposed by a spar mandates an increase in the support base. For some vessels—say, a shoal-draft fatty with a long, flat run of keel and stunted rig—all that is required is a few more jack stands. The deep draft, fin keel can be a very different story. Some yards simply refuse to store boats with spars in, or at least tightly control the types of vessels that are allowed such options. A winter gale and ice storm can severely test the quality of any support base. Some yards require clients storing their vessels with spars stepped to sign a release form protecting the yard from legal responsibility. It's questionable whether or not such an agreement would be upheld in a court.

If you are considering keeping your vessel's spar stepped during winter storage take a close look at the following questions. If the answer to each is yes, your idea is probably a viable alternative.

- Does the yard you have chosen allow storage with the mast stepped?
- Does the configuration of your vessel's hull allow for safe blocking support when the mast is stepped?
- Is your cradle or blocking system adequate to support the extra weight and windage aloft?
- Has the spar recently been removed and inspected?
- Will you be able to cover your vessel adequately with the spar in?
- Can all of the necessary repair and maintenance work be accomplished with the mast stepped?

If the idea still survives your scrutiny, there are a few hints worth keeping in mind. First of all, keep all standing rigging attached and reasonably tight. I have seen owners who like to release their vessel's lower shrouds because the winter cover fits better. This is just fine when an individual bids farewell to his or her sloop on a warm, Indian summer afternoon. Things will change in the fall gales that lie ahead. As the wind begins to howl, the spar starts a fore-and-aft oscillation, which does its best to shake the mast out of the boat, and the boat out of its supports. Even if neither of the former occurs, this movement will take a toll on hardware and standing rigging. Aboard my own boat I set up a detachable inner forestay and running backstays. I also prefer to remove all halyards and replace them with messenger lines. Ultraviolet radiation and acid rain have destructive effects on the synthetic polymers used in modern cordage.

THE BACKYARD BOATYARD

Hauling a boat out doesn't mean that it must be stored in a boatyard. In many areas there are independent boat transport companies willing to move your boat to any location you desire. Obviously, the larger the vessel and the longer the distance, the higher the price. The option isn't quite as cost effective in locations

Small boats are easily stored on their own trailers. With the proper equipment, even larger keel boats can be trailered.

where a boatyard must do the hauling and launching. The double handling erodes the savings attributed to less costly storage.

Still, many find that a backyard boatyard alternative is much to their liking. If you choose this option, a Brownell trailer may be able to deliver your vessel. Follow the guidelines suggested in Chapter 2 regarding regular boatyard blocking procedures. Screw jack stands are ideal blocking supports. Be sure the ground is firm and stable. It does not have to be paved. If there are any doubts about the ground on which the stands will rest, try putting plywood squares under each stand leg to increase the base area. Remember that most of the weight of the vessel should be transmitted to the ground via the keel, rather than through the jack stands at the hull support points. Once the vessel is in place, check to make sure that the supporting arrangement you have chosen will withstand gusty winds. Remember that while the vessel remains vertical relatively little stress is placed upon supporting side structures. If the boat starts to list, the loads change dramatically. Once a vessel starts to heel on land, there is neither buoyancy nor the righting moment of ballast working to correct the situation. Make sure that you have supported your boat in a manner that will keep it rock stable and plumb vertical on those squally winter nights.

BUDGET YARDS

The majority of boaters on tight budgets still opt for boatyard storage. They shop around, and place a low storage price at the top of their yard choice prerequisites. These folks are usually handy enough to take care of their own winterization and maintenance needs. They are willing to accept a yard that provides minimal services. In some areas, such facilities exist as a location rather than as a business. These are little more than parking areas for boats.

Location is indeed a big cost-saving factor. Some yard owners have capitalized on the simple fact that one finds lower rent in less appealing surroundings. One boatyard owner I know leases land next to a municipal sewer plant. The facility has the ambience of a holding tank, but is always booked to capacity. Another yard in the area had been plagued by burglary problems. The new owner's

Haulout at a commercial drydock sometimes beats the cost of yacht-oriented facilities.

wife raises dobermans; a very symbiotic business arrangement has evolved. Unfortunately, one customer took a late afternoon nap, slept through the closing of the yard, and awoke to a situation that made gales and lee shores seem benign!

The Collective

"It's a Commie pilot!" joked one old Down Easter. He was referring to the assemblage of some 20 boats, all in the 30- to 40-foot range, waiting for a big Grove hydraulic crane to haul them out for the season. The day before, their masts had been plucked out in a synchronized, well-planned operation. Each owner had assembled his own crew to disconnect electrical wires and antennas, remove booms, and loosen all but the last of the standing rigging; then the combined crews efficiently moved each spar to preset horses.

This was a group of owners who had banded together to carry the do-it-yourself spirit one step further. Harnessing their interest in hands-on involvement with their boats, as well as a desire to be cost effective, they had leased a piece of land, contracted with a crane operator, and organized their ranks into a pretty effective haulout operation. Their version of a yacht club focused on function rather than form. Instead of looking for a club house, they chose to invest in their own yard. They determined there was no need to purchase boat-handling equipment; a crane and operator could be hired for a few days in the fall and spring. (The collective did own a set of slings with a soundly constructed spreader bar arrangement.) The land they leased was filled with boats in the winter, and used in the summer as a parking lot by a busy nearby restaurant.

These people were willing to roll up their sleeves and go to work; they saved dollars by expending time and effort. A nucleus of old-timers annually introduced the few new members of the group to the skills of handling boats on land. There were annual spring and fall meetings during which plans and expenditures were agreed upon. The underlying principle was to keep things safe and simple.

There are dozens of reasons why similar efforts fail. I recall

Hydraulic cranes are a good choice for unstepping spars.

Electronic gear at the masthead requires careful handling.

two vivid episodes. In one situation a do-it-yourselfer, with many skills comparable to a pro, decided to haul a spar out of his yawl using a crane with too short a hoist height. To accommodate the large spar, the mast was attached to the hook at a point well below the center of balance. Sections of railroad iron were lashed as a counterbalance. As the crane lifted the spar out of the step and above the deck, a knot slipped, and one of the sections of iron plummeted into the cockpit, striking the compass binnacle. Damage was done but no one was hurt. Had the binnacle been the head of the person attempting to control the twisting spar, a real tragedy would have resulted. In another situation, a do-it-yourselfer hoisted a boat, placed it on a trailer, and then drove off, forgetting to move the crane boom. The hook caught the backstay, and the rig collapsed astern. The courts are having field days with cases involving gross negligence such as this.

For safe operation of a crane, not just any spot will do. There must be a well-structured bulkhead with enough water alongside to accommodate reasonable draft. The filled-in area behind the bulkhead must be able to bear both the weight of the crane and the weight of the vessel. If the hauled boats are to be "walked" to their storage area, stable ground and a crane of substantially larger capacity than the vessels being moved are essential.

Going It Alone

In a few cases, it is feasible to set up one's own hauling facility. The concept may appeal to those who own or have access to waterfront property. There is a variety of ways to get a boat up a beach and into the back yard. These range from outrageously costly to downright labor intensive.

The plank-and-roller method is a simple system that doesn't require too large a capital investment. It does require a well-made cradle, constructed of steel or heavy timber, with full-length, well-secured longitudinal bottom stringers. Heavy planks are laid out to form a course over a reasonably smooth beach face; on top of these planks go three-to-six-inch-diameter pipe rollers—about twice as many as you need to support the cradled boat. In places where the tidal range is at least as much as the draft of the boat to be hauled, the cradle is rolled down to the water at low tide and blocked into place. (Wooden cradles need to be adequately weighted down to prevent them from floating away.) At high water the vessel is carefully guided into the submerged cradle. Once the boat is aligned in the cradle, the dropping tide will do the next part of the operation. The boat is then coaxed up the beach by means of a stout block and tackle, powerful truck, or winching mechanism.

Many variables can complicate this otherwise simple system. Strong wind and sea conditions can spell disaster. The operation should definitely be attempted in a protected bay or on a calm day. If the cradle slips off its rollers, the day is wasted. Even if all goes well, the system is still brutally labor intensive.

If the material to construct a marine railway can be procured on a scrap basis, this may be a tempting alternative for the committed do-it-yourselfer. Under closer examination, however, the scheme nearly always proves to be economically unfeasible, as well as impractical in a number of other ways.

A backyard boatyard, complete with small marine railway. In the majority of cases, however, constructing one's own railway proves to be no bargain.

If you're interested, start by taking a close look at the intertidal zone your railway will traverse. Soft mud, uneven or rocky surfaces, and strong current and wave activity will rule out a site, as will an incline of more than 20 degrees. If conditions prove adequate, carefully investigate the design parameters required for safe hauling. For a railway sturdy enough to handle a full-keel, 30-foot sailboat on its cradle, you will need a railway carriage approximately 8 feet by 16 feet. Rails are normally set 5 to 8 feet apart. Wooden ties made from dimension timber at least 8 inches square should be set approximately every 15 feet, depending on the substrate and track gauge. Tally up what the rails, ties, carriage, and winching mechanism will cost, and add in the time you think it will take to construct the railway. There will almost certainly be welding involved, so unless you're skilled with a torch, better figure on additional expense for professional assistance at that stage in the operation. By the time you've added up materials and labor, you may find yourself taking a fresh look at the local yard prices.

THE DO-IT-YOURSELFER'S
WINTERIZATION SCHEDULE

The owner who maintains his own boat becomes a jack-of-all-trades, and most likely, the master of many. Although this is not a book aimed at detailing maintenance techniques, it is important to be specific about some of the tasks that lay ahead. Let's take a look at just what is involved in a do-it-yourself winter layup.

The experienced skipper begins the winter layup preparations before a vessel is hauled. The boat's water tanks are emptied and the fuel tanks filled. This keeps condensation from forming, and the fuel also prevents oxidation of the metal tank skin. Many owners wisely choose to pour a fungicidal chemical into the fuel. There is a form of algae which finds the sulfur compounds in diesel fuel quite nutritious. This floating biological population tends to clog filters. Regular use of "Bio-Bor," or a similar compound, will alleviate this problem.

In some cases it's best to unload a boat prior to hauling; in others, the opposite is true. Such decisions should be based on the logistics of how far you must carry your gear from the boat to the car. Don't forget to consider the effect of trips up and down the ladder. Those able to bring their boats alongside a dock are better off unloading as much gear as possible prior to hauling.

Make certain that you are aware of haulout procedures. These vary from yard to yard, and taking things for granted can lead to problems. In some facilities, the owner is expected to pilot his vessel into the railway cradle, travelift slipway, or crane slings. In other situations, this would not be allowed. I've been in yards where owners have joined in the stepping and unstepping process. In other places, including the yard I run, this is considered a hazard. There are usually good reasons for the policies that have evolved.

Once the boat is hauled and blocked, you may wish to combine a good external cleaning with an owner-performed survey. Start with a good wash and scrub of the decks, topsides, and underbody. Notice how well the deck drains as you hose down the boat. It's important that water not be trapped in areas downhill from scuppers. A properly blocked boat will have its waterline parallel with flat ground. Some cradle and keel configurations make this a difficult theory to put into practice. Once your boat is thoroughly washed and scrubbed, spend a little time waxing the topsides if you have a fiberglass boat. Acid rain, air pollution, and the chafe from a winter cover are no friends of the paint or gelcoat. A good coat of wax helps lessen their effect.

In areas where winter weather brings freezing temperatures, careful winterization is a must. Items that may freeze and burst need to be removed from the boat. Water systems, both fresh and salt, need to be drained completely, or filled with a non-toxic antifreeze solution.

The engine should be run with fresh water from a hose pumping through the raw water cooling system. After the proper running temperature is reached, the raw water pump pick-up hose can be moved to a bucket filled with antifreeze or methanol. Several gallons should be allowed to be sucked into the engine block and exhaust system.

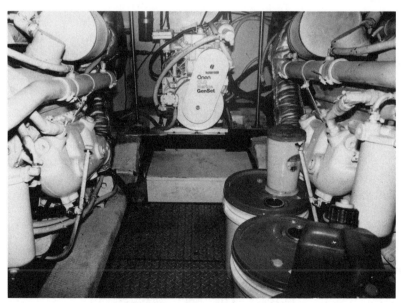

The winterization drill should include generator systems as well as the engine itself.

As a diesel engine is stalled out with the kill switch, a spray cylinder wall lubricant such as "Engine Stor" should be squirted directly into the air intake to protect the upper combustion chambers. If you have a gasoline auxiliary, spray in the lubricant until the engine stalls out of its own accord. Now check the antifreeze level in the fresh water side of the cooling system. Inexpensive gauges are available for this purpose. Next, the oil should be pumped out and all filters changed. A light lubricant spray should be placed on electrical contacts and other points prone to corrosion.

The ship's batteries usually need attention. Once all electric pumps have been winterized, drained, and/or filled with a non-toxic antifreeze, many owners remove the batteries. Some prefer to leave them in place and maintain their charge with a shore power converter. It's best to avoid trickle-charging. Lead-acid storage batteries prefer monthly applications of a higher current. Discharged cells are likely to freeze, damaging the internal plates as well as the casing.

Before leaving the boat closed for the winter, clean the bilge out. Sanitize, as well as winterize, the head. There are plenty of cleaners available in the supermarket capable of doing the job. I like to finalize the head cleaning ritual with a dose of Sudbury's marine toilet conditioner, which lubricates rubber seals, O-rings, and valves. Pour a cup of antifreeze into the bowl, and say goodbye until spring.

Holding tanks are another story, one which most yards don't want to hear about. Don't wait until you're on land to consider their contents. It's best to visit an operational pumpout station prior to hauling your boat. Empty the tank, at least to the extent possible. Add deodorizing conditioner and antifreeze and don't use it again until next season.

Water filters, hot water heaters, and accumulators are notorious for their tendencies to freeze and burst during the winter. Many professionals avoid these problems by blowing out water systems with compressed air, rather than adding non-toxic, terrible-tasting antifreeze. The do-it-yourselfer can try to drain each of these fixtures individually if necessary.

Don't forget a cup of antifreeze for the head. If necessary, consult manufacturers' specifications to make sure the antifreeze you use does not corrode the pump.

A covered boat has the best protection from the elements, but be sure that your boat is also well protected from the cover. Plastic tarps have become quite popular. They are waterproof, reasonably rugged, and quite inexpensive when compared to the alternative of fitted canvas. They are also nearly as abrasive as sandpaper and have ruined many a fine paint job. The secret to avoiding problems begins with proper installation. Be sure the cover is lashed in a manner that prevents it from moving excessively. Pad contact points when possible. Carefully check that the grommets are not in direct contact with the topsides. Last, oversized covers that can be brought down below the waterline can be tucked under jack stand pads. But close attention must be paid to how these are set up and secured.

Many marinas are covering their clients' boats with shrink wrap. The process has a cosmetic appeal, and applicators usually provide cowl-type ventilators to allow vital air circulation. Be sure that the applicator has a careful touch. I once had a cover wholesaler come by the yard to demonstrate his product. We chose a meticulously refinished antique mahogany runabout, spray

Inadequate covering is a waste of time and can do more harm than good. Abrasive plastic tarps left to flog and shred have ruined many a paint job.

Shrink wrap can produce a snug, dust-free cocoon or a catastrophe, depending on the skill of the applicator.

Clear reinforced plastic over a wood frame makes an effective, solar-efficient cover.

coated with multiple coats of a clear linear polyurethane finish. The plastic was rolled out, cut to size, and heat shrunk with a large propane torch. But some areas received too much heat. I'm sure the cover could withstand most gales, for the plastic had been fused to the bright finish of the topsides. As the demonstrator peeled back both the cover and the finish, all he could say was, "People varnish every spring, anyway." Beware of mixing big propane torches and fine finishes.

By the time you have winterized, covered, and cleaned your boat, you'll have a pretty good idea about what must be done before spring launching. Put an itinerary together before the winter months dull your memory. The next chapter details a systematic procedure for itemizing maintenance and refit chores that need to be attended to in order to ensure smooth sailing the following spring. Try to use those last Indian summer days to get a head start on the maintenance tasks that lie ahead.

6

Preparing For The Refit:
A Do-It-Yourself Maintenance Survey

M AKE NO MISTAKE: I am not suggesting that by reading this chapter you will become a competent, professional marine surveyor. The process I have outlined is a cursory examination that is meant to uncover problem situations. This may very well lead to the need for a qualified surveyor's evaluation. The purpose of this chapter is to provide boat owners with a cookbook approach to looking over a hull and the other vital components common to most vessels. Maladies discovered during the survey tend to fall into one of three categories. The first is cosmetic and includes any deterioration which does not stress the functional nature of the craft. Gouges in topside coatings, flaked and peeling varnish, and minor crazing in gelcoats are examples of cosmetic problems. The second category concerns structural problems. Examples are cracks in FRP laminates, severe interlaminer blistering, impact damage to hull/deck structures, and electrolysis of fastenings in a wooden boat. The third category is composed of safety-related shortcomings that present a potential hazard. Broken strands in standing rigging wire, deteriorated fittings that attach lifelines, and a badly corroded exhaust system are all examples of such safety concerns.

As you move through the procedure described below, jot down notes on any areas in question or use a tape recorder as you proceed. In some cases, you might even want to photograph an area and use these visual aids to better detail what you would like the yard to do.

Once a list of flaws has been compiled, a priority ranking process begins. Safety-related issues must be taken care of first. Certain structural problems, which are prone to rapid deterioration if not promptly attended to, also deserve early attention. This leaves a boat owner with a clear view of what separates repairs that would make his vessel look nicer from those that will make it safer and more seaworthy. In the end, it is the owner who decides how to deploy maintenance funds. If you keep these three categories of needs in mind, you'll be in a better position to make such refit decisions.

THE HULL

Every owner should do an annual stem-to-stern, inside-and-out inspection of his boat. If possible, look over your vessel immediately after it has been hauled out. Certain damage, such as that occurring on the foot of the keel from grounding, may not be easily seen after the vessel has been blocked up. Once the underbody has been pressure sprayed and is free from marine growth, closely inspect the character of the hull's surface. Take note of how well the antifouling paint has adhered. If your boat is fiberglass, check for blisters and mark large groupings or clusters. Records should be kept of the approximate number, size, and location of blisters to help determine whether or not the problem is worsening. At best, blistering is a sign of poorly anchored bottom paint. In many cases, the problem lies deeper in the gelcoat or the laminate itself. This has become a problem common for older, as well as relatively new, boats. The industry is in a turmoil over the issue, and all that seems to be agreed upon is if repairs are not carried out, the problem will continue to worsen. Those facing the prospect of such repairs should find professionals with a proven track record for coping with such dilemmas. Think seriously before tackling it on a do-it-yourself basis. Those who are familiar with plastic resins and putties may be able to achieve a self-cure. Those who haphazardly approach the issue can do more damage than they realize.

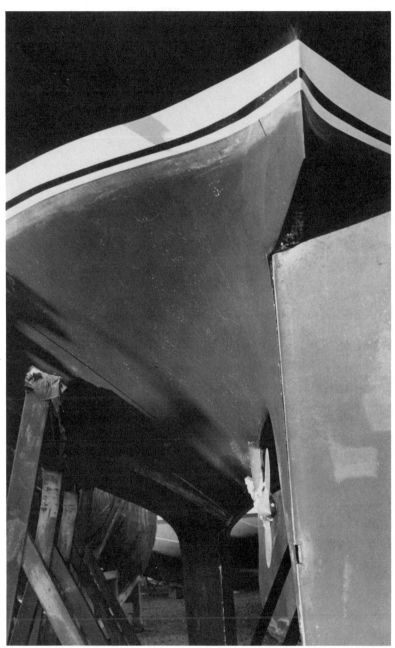

Begin your survey with a thorough inspection of the hull, including rudder and skeg, propeller shaft and blade, keel, and through-hull fittings.

Pay close attention to gelcoat condition both above and below the waterline. Check for blisters, and keep a record of their size, number, and location for future monitoring.

Look closely at deadwood/ballast seam. Cosmetic difficulties may be a sign of structural problems.

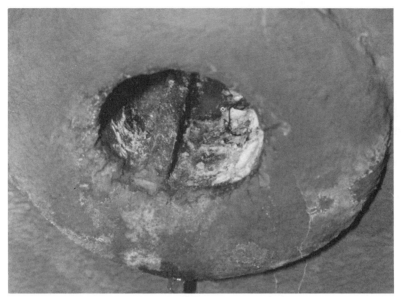

Inspect both ends of all through-hull fittings.

The hull inspection should also focus on points of high stress loads. Remember that the garboard region is continually being tensioned and compressed as the ballast keel resists heeling on one tack and then on the other. This tensioning and bending by opposing directions of force is known as reverse cycle loading and it imposes considerable strain on a hull. Older wooden boats tend to develop plank movement, and fastenings lose their grip. Fiberglass hulls with overly thin skins and poor structural framing may suffer from excessive flexing, a condition known as oil canning. This is a very serious problem since it tends to destroy the resin bond and greatly decreases the structural integrity, which has already proven inadequate. If serious crazing and cracking is visible in the gelcoat, a professional should be contracted to determine whether or not the damage extends to the laminate below. Cracks and crazing on rudder blades and near keel attachment points should also be closely scrutinized.

Through-hull penetrations are the next point of concern. Begin by scraping antifouling paint away from the fittings. Look for

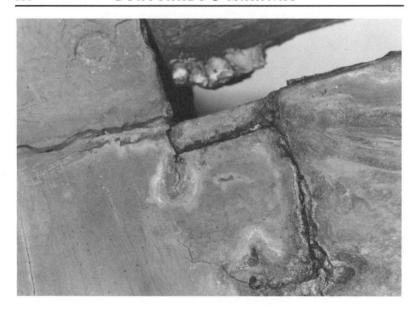

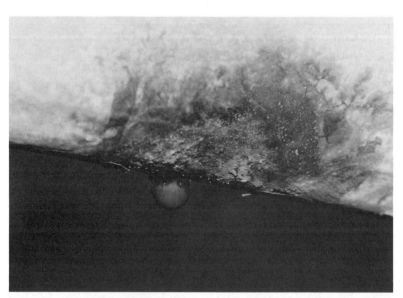

Rudders and rudder posts need careful attention. Top: Deterioration at the gudgeon should be closely inspected. Bottom: Oozing, rusty liquid at the end of this blade indicates potentially serious problems.

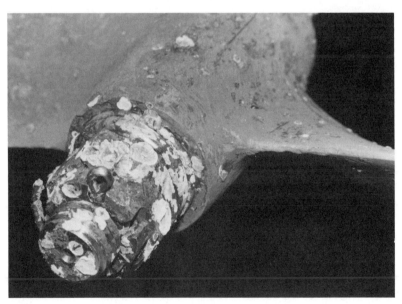

Top: *Severe electrolysis on propeller blade and shaft.* Bottom: *Look for signs of electrolysis on the castle nut and cotter pin.*

pink discoloration, a sign of electrolytic corrosion. If the hardware is pocked and eaten, replacement may be necessary. Don't neglect to check transducers, impellers, and other such devices. Rudder post apertures, as well as rudders themselves, should be carefully inspected. Above the waterline, problems may not sink a vessel, but they stand out rather plainly. Damage to topside gelcoat and laminate layers are normally easily repaired by a competent professional. Do-it-yourselfers usually go through quite a learning curve before their skill level reaches what is needed to hide a helmsman's mistakes.

The boat owner contemplating a better-than-new finish, comparable to an automotive paint job, should seek out the best professional spray facility in the area. Brush jobs, especially those done by a talented pro, can yield a mighty respectable finish, but not quite the same as a top-of-the-line spray job. We have never sold an Awlgrip spray topside job to a tugboat owner. On the other hand, many professional truckers choose linear polyurethane paint due to its superior durability, and boat owners also benefit from the rugged nature of this coating. The level of finish can vary without serious effect on overall durability. However, the cost of the final result is very much linked to the appearance factor; the greater the perfection, the higher the cost. For those with plank-on-frame wooden boats, urethanes will not give the best results. These high tech paints need a stable base for application, something the swelling and contraction of a planked boat won't allow.

The sheer region of your vessel is the next area to deserve close scrutiny. Remember, it is the junction of two major structural parts. Hull-to-deck joints are an engineering concern. Signs of movement, such as cracked or crazed FRP laminate, or even simple bedding problems at the toerail, should be checked carefully.

DECK

This area, including the coach roof and cockpit, needs a general going over. Deck delamination is a growing problem found in many fiberglass boats. By using a small tack hammer and gently tapping the surface of a laminate in question, you can quickly determine whether or not it is securely attached to the core material beneath. The structure should have a clear ring, rather than a dull, empty thud. If such problems are noticed, prompt attention may only require simple spot repairs. Left unchecked, these types of difficulties can evolve to the point where the entire deck must be replaced.

Penetrations through the deck and cabin house expose a cross section of laminate. Many reasonably well-made craft have suffered from such poorly sealed equipment installations. For example, when cabin portlights are fitted and not adequately bedded with caulking, water can find its way into voids and attack the exposed laminate cross section. I've seen plywood cabin coamings nearly destroyed by this problem. Leaks are not only a bane to those who occupy the accommodations below decks; they are serious threat to the structure itself.

Next, check to make sure lifelines are free from flaws. Handrails must be well fastened, and not prone to giving way at the time they are most needed. A 200-pound adult accelerated by the lurching motion of a powerful seaway can exert a considerable load on gear he may come into contact with. Be certain the structural integrity of your vessel suits the type of boating you will be doing. Those who sail summers on Long Island Sound have very different needs from those who set forth on an ocean passage to the Marquesas.

INTERIOR STRUCTURAL CONCERNS

Much can be concealed below decks. Builders tend to hide the inner hull skin nuts-and-bolts construction details behind a salty interior decor. Take time now to inspect obscure corners. Check how the chainplate attachment is holding up. Look in lockers and see if the glass work that holds bulkheads in place is still attached to the hull. Inspect floor frames, keel bolt pads, and the stuffing boxes for the propeller shaft and rudder post. This is the time to implement a stem-to-stern search. Shine a bright light on surfaces normally hidden. Inspect beneath the cabin sole and inside the overhead liner. Look closely for leaks in highly suspect areas, such as where portlights penetrate the cabin sides. The same diligence should prevail when inspecting the hull-to-deck joint from inside. Lifeline stanchion base plates, cleat fastenings, and other hardware attachment mechanisms are often responsible for small but annoying leaks.

Many of today's fiberglass production boats are built with a one-piece hull liner that hides the inner hull skin. Dropped into place before the hull-to-deck joint is sealed, the liner provides structural support and an instant interior layout. It does, however, make it exceedingly frustrating—sometimes virtually impossible— to gain access to vital structural members or hardware in need of attention. Sometimes the only choice is to cut through the hull liner. While this is not an option to be undertaken lightly, neither should it be avoided if the circumstances seem to warrant it. Perhaps one item on the refit list might be to install inspection plates for easier future access to crucial fittings.

STANDING AND RUNNING RIGGING

If staying afloat is a sailor's first priority, keeping the mast up ranks a close second. A variety of engineering forces are handled in the spar and the wire that holds it in place. Look at the arrangement with the understanding that one weak link can result in disaster. The situation is much like a series electrical circuit: one problem and all the lights go out. Each piece of hardware must be regularly inspected. Small fittings such as toggles, tangs, and swages need close scrutiny. Use a magnifying glass or a jeweler's loop to look for stress cracks, elongation, or any sign of deformation. If a clevis pin has elongated a hole in a toggle, make note to replace the fitting. Stainless steel 1 × 19 rigging wire is immensely strong and possesses very little stretch. However, don't let its shiny surface fool you. Wire that looks fine from a few feet away could be severely deteriorated. A broken strand, even though there may be 18 others left, means that the wire must be replaced. Running a piece of a nylon stocking over each shroud or stay is a good way to pick up burrs or cracks that otherwise might go unnoticed.

Take time to carefully look over your spar. While it is stepped,

Left: *When the spar is pulled, check the mast step for signs of deterioration.* Right: *Mast heel of a Nonsuch 36 unstayed spar. Check for signs of fatigue.*

check the alignment of the column, the rake, and the prebend. Observe the fore-and-aft, as well as athwartships, deviations from a straight line. Modern rigging technology allows for considerable sail control through spar bending. Be sure you understand the limits of what hydraulic loads can be imposed on your rig.

Inspect the tangs and spreader attachment mechanisms. Check the masthead welds and structures that hold spinnaker halyard blocks. Evaluate the condition of halyard sheaves and the halyards themselves. If there is excessive side play between a sheave and its side plates, this should be attended to. If a halyard were to jump the slot in the sheave, it could become wedged. Imagine if this occurred at 0300 in the midst of a Gulf Stream squall.

Spreaders and the important fittings associated with their attachment are often overlooked. I once heard a fellow, recently returned fom a winter in the Caribbean, say that it wasn't until the rot bloomed in his schooner's wooden spreaders that he noticed the problem. Alarmed by a green area on the underside of one of the cross trees, he climbed aloft and discovered the warm, moist,

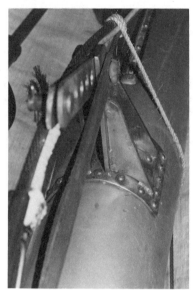

Left: *Carefully inspect stainless steel rigging wire. Broken strands mean the wire must be replaced.* Right: *Examine stainless steel welds for signs of working and discoloration.*

tropical climate had caused a plant growth to thrive on his schooner's timber spreaders. You may be glad to have alloy spreaders. Aluminum won't rot, but it can sustain serious corrosion. Some spar manufacturers have had a nasty habit of fastening aluminum hardware to stainless steel without adequate bedding or insulation material between. The dissimilar metals galvanically interact, and the aluminum begins to oxidize at an alarming rate. Left unchecked, this process can do considerable damage. Repair efforts should begin at the first sign of such corrosion.

Many alloy spreaders terminate with a mechanism designed to clamp the upper and/or intermediate shroud in place. If this structure is fabricated from aluminum, great care must be taken to isolate it from contact with the stainless steel shrouds it is meant to hold in place. Dissimilar metals are a problem in all marine applications. Spars are certainly no exception.

Winches and other labor-saving gear enhance the ability of

any halyard, sheet, or line handler. Like all mechanical equipment, these items need regular servicing. In addition to annual cleaning, lubrications, and corrosion checks, a sailboat owner should evaluate the functional nature of the hardware system aboard his vessel. In many circumstances poor performance results from the wrong piece of equipment or improper installation rather than equipment malfunction. It's better to install a system of winches, blocks, and other load-handling hardware too large, rather than too small. Overloading such equipment is dangerous and inefficient. When you look at the manufacturer's data for a given piece of equipment, note the difference between tensile strength data and working load recommendations. The latter is the figure one should use to calculate if a piece of gear is appropriate for the demands placed on it. In your survey, list deck hardware that should be moved or replaced.

ENGINES

Powerboaters tend to be highly aware of their engines; sailors tend to overlook them. Hidden away in a box or the bilge, the sailboat's auxiliary suffers from the old, "out of sight, out of mind" attitude. Owners expect blind obedience from the turn of a key, but are oblivious to their responsibilities toward maintenance. Many never read their owner's manual. But if you plan a functional preventive maintenance program you'll have far greater success with engine reliability.

At the end of the season, take a close look at the power plant. Start by searching for water leaks. Rust on iron, or a green stain on copper and bronze fittings, indicate that a seawater conduit is not sealed properly. A loose $2 clamp on a rubber hose can quickly lead to the demise of the $500 starter. Carefully check all hose clamp fittings. Look closely at the water pumps and be sure that the belts that drive them are neither too loose nor too tight. If there is excessive black residue, indicating frictional wear on the V-belt, make a note to replace the belt. The raw water pump should be opened up and inspected. Look for signs of deterioration of the

Major engine repairs happen less frequently if the oil is changed regularly and the cooling system is maintained.

Outdrive units need annual maintenance.

impeller. Replace it if its condition is at all questionable. An improperly cooled engine can seriously damage major mechanical parts.

Keep in mind that the engine is only one aspect of the propulsion system. The transmission, reduction gear, drive shaft, propeller, and associated hardware also need close scrutiny. Take a look around the engine compartment. Start with the raw water intake through-hull, and trace all associated engine plumbing. Look closely at the exhaust system. Are there signs of leaks? Establish whether the exhaust gases are carried in a water-jacketed pipe or are mixed with sea water from the cooling system at an injected elbow. Understanding how the system functions will help you anticipate where problems are likely to arise. An owner's manual can be quite an asset in this endeavor.

If your boat's engine is an unfamiliar cast iron configuration, consider having the yard mechanic do a fall checkout for you. You may already have hired him to winterize the engine, change oil and filters, and decommission the mechanical equipment. While he is there, have him give the whole system a close look. Describe any idiosyncrasies you've noticed during the season. Marked changes in operating temperature, oil pressure or charging behavior usually indicate something needs investigation. Many problems can be cleared up while still in their early stages, usually resulting in a significantly less dramatic bill.

ELECTRICAL SYSTEMS

Electricity in a boat is a small step away from electricity in the water. The electrician's efforts focus on keeping current flowing where it is wanted and avoiding what is called stray current pathways. When a submersible bilge pump is wired improperly, and its positive conductor is exposed to the moisture normally associated with this part of the boat, a series of dilemmas arise. Electrons flow in new directions—often through the shaft, strut, and other underwater metal surfaces. Stray current corrosion is the most active form of electrolysis and destroys more metal than any other version. However, it can be avoided through proper wiring, the mainstay of a good marine electrical system.

Spend time and get to know where the wires are routed on your own vessel. Look at their origins and terminations. Are there clean metal terminals, or is there a green oxide coating the surface? If so, either the owner or a competent electrician must sooner or later come to grips with the problem. The do-it-yourselfer, comfortable with Ohm's Law and familiar with the use of a multimeter, can do quite a bit to rectify the shortcomings of a deteriorated electrical system. If you are unsure of what to do, call in a pro and hire him to evaluate the system and make appropriate recommendations.

PLUMBING

Plumbers may not have a romantic trade, but they do laugh all the way to the bank. Ashore we tend to dial a phone number and forget about our plumbing problems, at least until the bill arrives. Aboard our boats it can be a different story. Plumbing failures have ruined many a cruise. Learning how to handle these emergencies is part of the apprenticeship to being a veteran sailboat owner. Perhaps the traditionalist's fondness for a cedar bucket is the answer; at least the equipment hasn't been tagged with legislation requiring connection to a holding tank or a macerator pump. Unfortunately, the technology is a little too primitive for most sailors and their guests; consequently a variety of seats, bowls, pumps, and pipes have been called upon to fill the gap. Your initial encounter with all this may be civilized, but when things go astray the repair episodes can make cedar bucket handling seem refined.

A friend of mine avoids the marine head blues by annually rebuilding his boat's head. He finds that "like new" pumping capabilities are worth maintaining. Another fellow I know carries a complete spare; if problems arise, a direct replacement is available. These plumbing-conscious sailors have probably been traumatized by a breakdown at some particularly intolerable time. The time to work on a head is when it is not needed, and when it has been pumped clean with a mild solution of chlorine bleach.

More boats sink due to bad plumbing than because of poor hull construction. All through-hull fittings at or below the waterline present a serious concern. There should be a shut-off valve located as close to the hull penetration as possible. The hoses involved in moving water to various parts of the vessel must have a substantially reinforced wall and be secured with tight-fitting hose clamps. At the end of the season, check for signs of deterioration. Rust around the clamp screws often signifies that it is time to replace these fittings. Many owners and builders prefer to double clamp all raw water hose connections below the vessel's resting and sailing waterline. At this time, look closely at the hoses themselves. If they have become too soft, they will tend to collapse as water is siphoned through them. This can be a major contributor to hard-to-find engine cooling problems.

Remember that pumps, tanks, fixtures, etc. are continually progressing toward breakdown. Those who opt for more complex systems must accept the responsibility of more extensive and expensive maintenance responsibilities.

PRIORITIZING

To complete your list, jot down the items that seem to have fallen between the cracks. It's a good time to remember the box needed for the binoculars or the fact that the galley sink only seemed to drain on one tack and not the other. If the hinge on the cockpit lazarette is missing screws, write it down. Do your best to get it all in writing. It is an arduous task, but it will pay off in the overall refit process.

Next you must determine what to do with all this data. Start by organizing the categories. The first focus is on the safety and structural aspects. This "must do" list would include anything from a hole below the waterline to a broken masthead fitting. Segregate these items and address the issue of getting the work done in a manner appropriate to your own particular circumstances. If you intend to have the work professionally handled, make sure the yard you have chosen understands the details of your worklist. If you are a do-it-yourself oriented individual, you have to decide if these tasks fall within your skill range.

The second category addresses the cosmetic issues. The priority given to each task on this list is a matter of your own discretion, but be sure to check closely to see that there are no serious structural items included that should have been listed in the previous category.

The last segment of your profile includes all items noted but not included as part of this season's refit priorities. None of these should be a threat to the structure or safety of the vessel. Presumably, these will be addressed at a later date and are not included at the moment, due to time or financial considerations. It is better to acknowledge and postpone a maintenance need than to simply ignore its existence altogether.

The following checklist has been compiled in order to provide boat owners with a handy means of performing their own maintenance surveys. It will help to organize a vessel's refit needs and develop a prioritized list.

MAINTENANCE SURVEY

• HULL •

Condition of surface below the waterline:
- ☐ blisters
- ☐ bottom paint
- ☐ impact damage
- ☐ structural concerns (cracks, crazing, seams)
- ☐ ballast keel, deadwood, centerboard

Hull fittings and running gear:
- ☐ through-hulls
- ☐ stern tube
- ☐ cutlass bearing
- ☐ strut
- ☐ shaft
- ☐ propeller
- ☐ zincs

Rudder, skeg, and attachment hardware:
- ☐ blade (cracks, crazing)
- ☐ post
- ☐ pintles and gudgeons
- ☐ glasswork

Comments:

• TOPSIDES •

Structural damage to fiberglass, wood, etc.:
- ☐ condition of gelcoat or paint
- ☐ boottop (blistering, etc.)
- ☐ rub strake
- ☐ toerail or caprail
- ☐ bulwarks
- ☐ problems at sheer
- ☐ cove stripe
- ☐ lettering

Comments:

• DECK •

Structural issues:
- ☐ delamination of core/FRP decks
- ☐ excessive flexing
- ☐ damage at stanchion bases
- ☐ rot
- ☐ deterioration of glue joints
- ☐ condition of hatches, wash boards, coamings, etc.
- ☐ winch bases
- ☐ cracks and crazing in FRP laminate
- ☐ other problems

Cosmetic concerns:

- ☐ condition of paint and gelcoat
- ☐ nonskid surface
- ☐ brightwork (sealer/varnish)
- ☐ portlights
- ☐ hatches
- ☐ other concerns

Deck fittings and hardware:

- ☐ signs of overloading
- ☐ broken gear
- ☐ incorrectly installed equipment
- ☐ hardware needing replacement
- ☐ hardware needing seasonal maintenance
- ☐ new gear to be fitted
- ☐ specific winch/track/block/cleat data

Comments:

• RIGS AND RIGGING •

Masts and spreaders:

- ☐ stepped: check column alignment
- ☐ unstepped: check for corrosion (close look at heel), dents, abrasion, soft wood, etc.
- ☐ spreader condition
- ☐ spreader fittings (inboard and outboard)
- ☐ condition of masthead welds and structure
- ☐ mainsail track
- ☐ tangs

Standing/running rigging:

- ☐ condition of wire, terminals, turnbuckles, toggles, clevis pins
- ☐ check halyards, blocks, and sheave boxes
- ☐ gear to be moved or replaced
- ☐ new gear to be installed

Lights and electronic equipment:

- ☐ broken gear
- ☐ condition of electrical wire in spar
- ☐ moisture problems

• INTERIOR STRUCTURAL INSPECTION •

Hull:

- ☐ stress cracks and crazing
- ☐ signs of delamination at bulkheads
- ☐ damage at chainplates, keel bolts
- ☐ floor frame delamination
- ☐ rudder post stress damage

Deck head and coach roof:

- ☐ signs of excessive movement
- ☐ damage from leaks
- ☐ delamination and deterioration of plywood
- ☐ hull-to-deck joint problems
- ☐ other complications

• PROPULSION SYSTEM •

Check shaft from stuffing box to coupling flange

Check for oil leaks in reduction gear and transmission

Check for engine oil leaks

Inspect engine mounts

Change and/or check:

- ☐ Oil
- ☐ Filters
- ☐ V-belts
- ☐ Pump impellers

Check for fuel leaks

Look for water leaks

Inspect exhaust system

Check raw water strainer and associated plumbing

Look over starter and engine-associated wiring

Comments:

• PLUMBING •

Ship's water supply:
- ☐ check from tank to pump
- ☐ inspect pump
- ☐ look for signs of water or air leaks
- ☐ check faucets, and service hand pumps
- ☐ change filters

Through-hull fittings and drains:
- ☐ trace all hose leads and inspect host clamps
- ☐ test, grease, and service through-hull shut-off valves
- ☐ list hardware to be replaced
- ☐ look for raw water leaks

Head and MSD equipment
- ☐ integrity of through-hull fittings and hose
- ☐ check for leaks and corrosion
- ☐ tighten hose clamps

Additional issues:

• ELECTRICAL •

Test function or main shut-off switch

Look for oxidized terminals and corroded bus bars

List equipment malfunctions

Check wire harnesses for chafe

Estimate water damage problem

Check lead acid batteries with hygrometer

Check back side of exposed instrument panels

List malfunctions of electronic equipment

Comments:

• COSMETIC CONCERNS BELOW DECKS •

Paint and brightwork problems

Upholstery maintenance

Problems with cabinetry

Alterations to accommodations

Lighting

Galley equipment

Installation of new gear

Other:

• NOTES ON UNDEFINED ISSUES •

7

Agreements, Estimates, Contracts, and Work Orders

Y ARD ADMINISTRATORS CAN make a one-man-band seem idle. Those boat owners who casually, "Oh, by the way," mention their refit needs while the manager is in the midst of taking the keel off an IOR boat scheduled for a big weekend race shouldn't be surprised if a few details are missed along the way. A more formal approach usually results in more complete follow-through. Request a meeting, write out the details and develop a mutually acceptable approach.

Let's assume you have done your investigative research, and have come up with a yard and a staff you feel at home with. The sailing season is headed into the shorter days of early fall, and it is time to put together plans for winter storage and repairs. You have made an appointment to meet with the yard manager and have already received the storage information, which the yard publishes each season. Prior to going to the meeting, you have calculated what the hauling/storing/launching fees will be. You know what it will cost to have the mast unstepped, and stored. You also note that the cradle the builder supplies with your boat will do nicely for winter storage, saving the cost of jack stands. However, in the yard's à la carte option list you have noticed that there will be a summer storage fee for the cradle. There is no free lunch. The final number for the winter storage is about what the neighboring yards are charging. However, the reason you are interested in this yard is simple: their craftsmen deserve the title. It's time to have a major

The bill of fare at this full-service yard reads like a refit list in itself.

paint job done, along with several repairs, and this is where quality results will be obtained.

You should arrive at the yard prepared. The survey technique described in the previous chapter should give you a realistic understanding of what the refit will entail; the meeting you are headed to will clarify the details. During this first meeting with yard management do a little talking and lots of listening. Be sure you clearly depict your boat's needs. Then let the yard representative detail your options. His approach may differ from what you had in mind. Quite often the learning curve the professional has gone through leads to insights an owner never realizes. It's more than likely that the yard staff has performed a similar refit on other vessels quite like your own. Inquire about such experience, and discuss the ways these refits were approached. Remember, there is nothing wrong with asking questions. It is important that the professional's response be clearly understood.

If you are constrained by a limited budget, make sure this is mentioned. There's nothing wrong with asking, "What is it going to cost?" The boat yard professional likes to clarify dollar details as early in a refit as possible. Certain work may be flat-rated and can be discussed at the first meeting. Other jobs may need to be inspected by a craftsman before an estimate can be made. There are a few situations where the extent of a repair cannot be ascertained until the system is dismantled. Even in these scenarios, however, a rough range of prices can still usually be discussed.

ESTIMATES

Estimates are a controversial issue. Most boating consumers see them as a vital part of their budget planning process. Yard administrators have mixed feelings. In many cases, fixed estimates are easily given, but some situations require a more flexible approach. Basically, the issue boils down to whether or not the full extent of the work involved in a refit can be determined prior to beginning the work. For example, linear polyurethane spray refinishing tends to involve surface areas that can be closely scrutinized prior to beginning the process. This places most of

With Awlgrip jobs, potential problems are visible from the start. Yards experienced in this kind of work often feel comfortable giving fixed estimates.

what will be labor intensive constraints in easy view. Cracked, peeling gelcoat, which must be entirely removed prior to painting, is visible from the start. The applicator knows what he is in for, and the manager, who must establish cost factors, sees where the time will go. Yards that have had several years of experience with LPU paints often feel comfortable enough with the process to give a fixed estimate on most jobs, based on flat-rate, per-foot pricing. Obviously, boats with seriously damaged surfaces or other unusual maladies cannot be handled with such an estimating process.

The opposite is true in the case of mechanical problems. Time and time again, a boat owner brings in a vessel with what seems to be a simple dilemma. The malfunction he refers to actually turns out to be a symptom of a much more complex shortcoming. In order to cure the apparent problem, a major repair of the entire system must be undertaken. Troubleshooting costs can grow quickly.

I recall two situations that occurred in a yard at the same time; both had to do with the replacement of small gasoline auxiliary engines. One owner chose to replace his tired power plant with a new diesel. The second owner hoped to avoid the expense of a new purchase and associated engine room modifications by installing a "more or less partially rebuilt" engine. In the first case, the yard routinely installed the new diesel, adapting engine beds, fuel tank, and exhaust system to suit the new engine, and the owner spent a happy summer sailing and motoring on Long Island Sound. The second owner's summer was plagued by engine problems. They were of a major, rather than a minor, nature. Mysteriously, the "somewhat rebuilt" engine allowed water to enter the cylinders. Both the exhaust system and the engine were pressure-tested. Three mechanics took their turn at diagnosing the problem, but no explanation of the leak was discovered. The shortcut proved to be the wrong choice. Most professionals agree that since so much of the cost of a rebuilt engine is labor, it's imperative to be sure that the resulting repair will offer long-term reliability. The logic favoring replacement can be quite compelling.

Estimates for engine replacement are readily available. But they are seldom flat-rated, for each vessel is to some extent unique.

With engine repairs, seemingly simple complaints often lead to complex and expensive overhauls. Fixed estimates are virtually impossible to give.

I have seen sisterships from the same mold vary by a factor of over 50% in engine installation cost. Ironically, the dollar difference had nothing to do with the engine itself; it was strictly a factor of an overstuffed engine room. One owner felt it necessary to have two alternators, a mechanical refrigeration system, a water maker, and a hydraulic autopilot drive system in the confines of an already inaccessible engine space. The engine removal and installation was relatively simple once the time-consuming process of removing the peripheral gear was taken care of. Yard managers like to have a good look at individual installations before even offering a ballpark estimate.

Some owners prefer to take their boats to several yards for estimates. This type of comparison shopping may or may not be cost effective. Keep in mind the factor of quality. The best job and the lowest price seldom go hand-in-hand.

Surveyors

In situations where major structural repairs are to be undertaken, a third party professional survey is well warranted. Insurance companies like the idea of a third party diagnosis. The owner benefits by having someone other than the supplier of the service detailing what is to be done.

For a survey to be of value, however, the surveyor must be competent and unbiased. All too often a boat owner asks a broker or repair yard to recommend a surveyor: in some situations it's like asking the fox to count the chickens. Word-of-mouth recommendations from a number of fellow boat owners are in most cases your most reliable guide to quality. Remember, however, that not all surveyors are equally competent in all fields. A surveyor accustomed to doing engine evaluations may not be the best choice for a major hull repair. For more detailed information on how to locate a quality surveyor, see *What Shape Is She In?* by Allan H. Vaitses (International Marine Publishing Company, 1985).

A copy of the survey may be helpful to the yard staff in preparation for the repair process. If the work involves major structural alterations to the boat, it may be advantageous to have the surveyor return while the work is in progress to verify the quality of repairs. In many cases, laminates and other structural fabrications are covered up with cosmetic coatings. A surveyor can more accurately judge a repair if he is present while the structural aspects are still open to view.

SCHEDULING AND CONTRACTS

Once the scope of a refit and the cost factors have been identified, a time frame and payment schedule should be discussed. Many misunderstandings are based upon these issues. An owner should clarify his desires regarding the date he hopes to relaunch in the spring; or, if the repair must be made in mid-season, the period he expects to be without the use of his boat. If this seems unrealistic given the scope of the refit involved, the yard manager should make this clear to the owner. The overcommitted yard tends to juggle commitments and may not be able to meet deadlines. If the time factor is very important, make sure that any work contract you sign contains a completion date and perhaps even a penalty clause. Keep in mind that overtime labor necessary to meet a deadline is usually passed on to the customer. Whenever possible, schedule work for a less busy time or when you can leave your boat with a yard for a lengthy period. There may even be a cost incentive to scheduling a refit at off-peak times. Discuss the possibility with the yard administrator.

The paperwork involved in scheduling a refit varies from yard to yard, and there is no correlation between the explicit nature of a contract and the thoroughness of the work that results. Some of the best yards I have seen sign an agreement with a handshake. Others produce documents akin to the UN Charter. (If you rely on a verbal agreement, it's a good idea to follow up with a letter designating refit details.) There are different ways of doing business, and it's important to feel comfortable with the yard you choose. Usually, larger operations tend to be more formal with their contractual agreements. Many facilities data process work orders. Software programs that track labor hours and integrate them directly with inventory and accounts receivable information are gaining in popularity. As with any computerized system, the result of this increased efficiency is increased formality.

A good written agreement often protects both parties. Costs, work to be done, and time frame, as well as other conditions, are spelled out clearly. A boatyard usually devises a form that details what its commitments are and what the flat rate fees will be. The document may also incorporate estimates on tentative work orders. Each owner should check the details and be sure that both parties are in agreement about task descriptions and dollar amounts. If the cost is billed on a time-and-material basis, the boat owner should have previous experience with—or great faith in—the facility he has chosen.

Written agreements deserve close scrutiny. They tend to be binding, and are usually literally interpreted by a court of law. Don't sign something you disagree with. Be sure that you have read the small print and understand what is being delineated.

Favored Status

Good customers tend to benefit in the long run. They are the regulars who stick with a familiar yard. They don't switch their allegiance to other facilities because paint is two dollars less a gallon. They tend to be as interested in the outcome of the work done on their vessels as they are in what it costs. These boat owners know how to communicate with yard personnel, and their efforts do not go unnoticed. Favored customer status prevails in every industry; boatyards are no exception. The thick wallet approach of the big tipper is one way of seeking priority status. But the owner who knows what he or she is doing and gets along with fellow boat owners, as well as the yard staff, is a welcome addition to any boatyard.

Paying bills promptly has a lot to do with maintaining good customer status. And monthly statements should not hold any surprises. Each customer, prior to signing any agreement, needs to understand how the yard's billing process works. It can vary greatly from one facility to another. For example, some yards expect full payment of hauling/storing/launching charges as soon as the boat is hauled. Others bill a portion in the fall and the rest in the spring. Work done on major refits usually results in progress payment statements being issued at the end of each month. Some yards require 1/3 of a fixed price prior to beginning the work, another 1/3 at the midway point, and the final 1/3 on completion.

Boatyards are always concerned about being left with a half-finished boat and a bankrupt owner who has skipped town. When this happens the yard must file a mechanic's lien, which in most states is a slow, paper-ridden process. Eventually the vessel can be sold at auction, and the yard may possibly be able to recoup some of what it is owed. The process varies from state to state and can take several years to complete. Meanwhile, the vessel remains unclaimed, unattended, and deteriorating. This is one reason why yard owners are often quite skeptical about major refits on older boats.

Keeping Records

A wise owner keeps a refit file. Included are his own end of season survey notes, the professional survey report (if one has been conducted), work agreements, and estimates and contracts pertaining to work being done on the vessel. He may even have photographs documenting pre- and post-repair status. In addition, monthly statements are kept in the file, as well as any other relevant material associated with the refit. Many jobs require clarification of specific issues. These amendments are best done in written form, with copies kept to update the file. All too often confusion arises over such details and how they affect the original agreement. It's important to address such questions when they first arise, not several months later after the details have been attended to.

All this documentation may seem excessive. It's true that if all goes as planned, the file will become little more than a scrapbook. But if things start to go astray, the file may prove to be a very useful reference source. There is nothing like signed written documentation when it comes to looking back at what should have been done, and what it should have cost. Quite often, irrefutable written agreements keep small misunderstandings from escalating into adversarial proceedings. In many situations the boat owner can refer to such documentation and avoid verbal accusations which benefit neither party.

AVOIDING UNPLEASANTRIES

The owner of a nearby yard once called me, asking if I had seen a stout wooden ketch which had recently been at his yard undergoing major structural repairs, the result of a serious collision. During the winter a new stem and bowsprit had been fitted, and other structural carpentry work was completed. In early spring, the yard manager and the owner agreed that dry, warm weather was not kind to a wooden boat. The vessel was launched, but her sails would remain in the loft until payment was made. The night after the skipper received his insurance check, he slipped the docklines and motored away on the tide. The yard was left with a set of tanbark sails and a large unpaid bill. Similar tales are told in many yards up and down the coast. An unscrupulous owner can leave a yard with a major problem. Inflexible early payment policies are enacted in the wake of such experiences, and responsible clients must shoulder the burden.

On the other side of the coin exist the accounts of owners who have been overbilled and their vessels abused, rather than repaired. There are tales of boats dropped, damaged and, in general, mishandled. These leave the industry's reputation tarnished and owners justifiably concerned. Fortunately such horror stories are infrequent exceptions to the rule. But unpleasantries of a more routine nature can and do occur.

Cost overrides can be a big problem. Despite efforts to keep within an estimate, there are situations where labor and material factors significantly exceed original assumptions. The causes of the override can range from a misconception over the extent of a repair to incompetence on the part of those doing the work. The owner facing the prospect of escalating repair costs must make difficult decisions. He or she may choose to refuse to pay more— and the yard may refuse to continue to work on the boat. In such strained circumstances legal recourse comes to mind. If at all possible, it's best to resolve the impasse before it reaches that level.

Basically, the owner needs to get to the bottom of what has caused the increased cost. Each situation will differ. If quality workmanship has prevailed, the fact should be noted. If a more extensive repair has evolved out of what seemed to be a lesser problem, this too should be taken into consideration. If it seems that the blame lies in an unrealistic initial estimate, an owner may justifiably become defensive, but if it turns out that hidden damage, unobservable at the time of the estimate, is the culprit, he or she needs to be more understanding.

An equitable solution begins with a recognition of who is financially responsible. Once the cause of the override has been determined, the parties must negotiate a compromise, an equitable means of dividing the costs between the boat owner and the boatyard. This step is often a difficult one. Most yards are willing to incur a fair share of the financial responsibility; it's bad publicity not to. They realize that occasionally mistakes are made, either in the estimating process or in the implementation phase of a refit. Their price structuring takes into consideration such contingencies. Within reason, they prefer to get the mistake resolved and press on with successful completion of the refit. Most owners benefit from such professionalism. A few fail to recognize fair treatment and push the issue beyond what is reasonable.

In situations where one or both parties remain inflexible, and a mutually acceptable solution cannot be reached, there is still an alternative to litigation: third party arbitration. This can be an informal approach, whereby the parties involved hire an independent marine surveyor who comes in and evaluates the circumstances that have led to the confrontation. His findings are not binding, but in many cases, he resolves the problem, simply by removing variables clouded by bias and innuendo. If a more formal approach to arbitration is desired, there are companies providing such services. One advantage to such processes lies in the fact that they tend to be less costly and more expeditious than courtroom battles. Again, I must stress that situations calling for such extreme measures are rare. Boatyard-related misunderstandings are usually much easier to resolve. Casual, but thorough, communication normally prevails.

8

Caring for Your Mooring

A MOORING SHOULD BE a conservative device. Overkill is the best design parameter, and regular inspections are essential. Even the most tranquil bay is constantly in motion. Tides and currents tug at the hardware, and over a prolonged period considerable wear results. Abrasion, like erosion, does not show its effect overnight. Time of expected use is one of the significant variables that must be compensated for in the ground tackle's original specification. For example, those whose moorings are seasonally launched, hauled, and inspected may not need to opt for hardware as heavy as do those who plan to leave their gear in the water year round.

Oceanographic considerations are another important factor. Water depth, tidal range, bottom substrate, and the exposure of the basin all dictate what it will take to keep your boat where it belongs. Meteorological patterns also have to be considered. In the U.S., the boating season coincides with the slack pressure gradients found on summertime weather maps. Lows tend to be less frequent and weaker, passing well north of major boating areas. Many boat owners think most often of the high frequency of calms that prevail in places like Long Island Sound and Chesapeake Bay. If the scantlings of your mooring gear are based only on such light air conditions, you may find your vessel in real trouble during early spring frontal passages, or in the grip of a fall hurricane. Like the offshore sailor who chooses his gear with the worst conditions in

The most desirable mooring areas offer 360-degree protection.

mind, a mooring purchase or rental should be done with a clear picture of how bad the bay can become.

The hardware involved in mooring tackle can vary considerably. In many areas, conventional mushroom anchors have been upstaged by less expensive engine blocks, slabs of concrete, and even augur-like mechanisms, which are screwed into highly compacted bottoms. Poking through the aftermath of a severe storm leads to some interesting feedback about such equipment. A few years ago, a helicopter crane was used in Marion, Massachusetts to extract 40 or 50 vessels blown ashore during Hurricane Gloria. It seems a chain reaction was the most significant factor in the disaster. A vessel to windward of most of the fleet, moored to a chunk of scrap iron and concrete, began to drag. During its traverse to leeward, it snagged other boats' ground tackle, collided with them, or caused other boats to intertwine their mooring cables. Perhaps as many as 20 boats came to grief, primarily due to the poor ground tackle of this one. From this lesson, and others like it, one can readily see the importance of being in a mooring area where there is tight control over hardware. Annual inspections benefit all involved.

MUSHROOM ANCHORS

Moorings are usually rather short-scoped ground tackle. Consequently, much larger anchor weights are needed. Conventional mushroom anchors are usually the most effective way to meet this requirement. The lip of the cast iron bell tends to dig into the substrate and offer mechanical holding power as well as brute weight. Devices such as shankless blocks of concrete need to be many times heavier than a mushroom anchor to secure a boat of identical size. These blocks have poor mechanical holding power and tend to be more easily dragged over bottoms, with the exception of oozy mud. They also tend to be more buoyant, due to their lower density than a cast iron anchor. In addition, a mushroom anchor that starts to drag is more likely to reset itself than is a block of concrete marching to leeward.

Inspected well-set-up mushroom moorings ready for launch. (John Hickey's Bay Marine, Oyster Bay, New York)

Corroded eye at the upper end of a mushroom anchor.

Cast iron mushroom anchors deteriorate in water and must be inspected regularly. Oxidation occurs to a greater or lesser extent, depending on the dissolved oxygen content of the water. In soft mud bottoms, where the sulfur content is high, other types of chemical deterioration can be a concern. The most active corrosion areas are at the eye provided for the chain shackle and at the lower end of the rolled steel shank, where it connects to the cast iron bell. Most mushroom anchor failures originate from deterioration at these locations.

It's difficult to arrive at a hard and fast table of anchor weights for a given size vessel. Secondary variables, such as exposure, composition of the bottom, weather patterns, and swinging room, play a significant role. Average conditions yield tables such as the one below. They are meant to be a starting point. If your vessel will be moored in an area with a hard, compact substrate, which prevents a mushroom anchor from burying itself, an increase in the recommended poundage would be wise. Deviation from average conditions in any of the variables tends to suggest the need for an increase in anchor weight. Keep in mind that no vessel has ever dragged to shore because its mooring anchor was too heavy.

TYPICAL WEIGHTS AND DIMENSIONS FOR MUSHROOM ANCHORS AND CHAINS.

Boat Length (feet)	Mushrom Anchor	Bottom Chain (galvanized)	Top Chain (galvanized)	Line	Chain	Pennants Stainless Steel Wire
under 16'	75 lbs.	5/16"	5/16"	1/2"	5/16"	1/4"
16–18'	100 lbs.	5/16"	5/16"	1/2"	5/16"	1/4"
19–22'	150 lbs.	3/8"	5/16"	5/8"	5/16"	1/4"
23–26'	200 lbs.	3/8"	5/16"	5/8"	5/16"	1/4"
31–34'	300 lbs.	1/2"	3/8"	3/4"	3/8"	1/4"
35–37'	350 lbs.	1/2"	3/8"	3/4"	3/8"	1/4"
38–40'	400 lbs.	1/2"	3/8"	3/4"	3/8"	1/4"
41–50'	500 lbs.	5/8"	1/2"	1"	1/2"	3/8"
51–60'	600 lbs.	5/8"	1/2"	1"	1/2"	3/8"
61–75'	750 lbs.	3/4"	1/2"	1"	1/2"	3/8"
76–100'	1000 lbs.	3/4"	1/2"	1"	1/2"	3/8"

THE CONNECTING LINKS

Shackles are the next link in the mooring tether. Normally a large-diameter shackle is affixed to the eye at the top of the mushroom shank. It's important to be sure that the screw type clevis pin will not inadvertantly loosen and drop out. Tightening is not enough. Shackle pins should be wired shut, spot welded, or peened with a hammer to prevent loosening. A smaller shackle, the maximum size the chain will accept, is then attached to the larger shackle at the upper end of the anchor shank.

Don't skimp on the quality of your shackles. At first it may seem that such a simple device must not vary too greatly from one manufacturer to another. To the contrary, the strength and durability of a shackle are greatly affected by the quality control during the manufacturing process. Galvanized, weldless, drop-forged steel shackles manufactured by Crosby or Wilcox-Crittenden are the standard of the industry. Oriental imitations, marketed at half the price, are a dangerous bargain.

Swivels are the weakest link in sound mooring design. Tidal currents and wind shifts cause moored boats to swing around in a circle. Without a swivel the chain kinks as the rotation continues. Swivels are most vulnerable at the pin and eye junction point. Close scrutiny of this articulated joint is an important part of good maintenance. I prefer to place the swivel between the top chain and a lower section. If the lower or bottom chain is long enough to be hoisted to the surface, the swivel can be checked without the need for pulling the mushroom anchor.

I prefer eye-to-eye swivels over jaw-and-eye swivels. The latter system does save the use of an extra shackle; however, it must rely on a fragile cotter pin to hold the clevis pin in place. Electrolysis and abrasion can destroy the cotter pin and allow the clevis pin holding the chain to slip out, resulting in disaster. As with any shackle used, proper seizing, welding, or other means of secondary security should be added. Once again, weldless, galvanized, drop-forged steel swivels manufactured by Wilcox-Crittenden are examples of what competitors attempt to copy.

In water over 30 feet deep, many boaters choose a combination of chain and nylon for their mooring anchor rode. The nylon

Note excessive play in the lower left swivel.

For deepwater moorings, three-strand nylon line is often used in combination with chain.

top pennant keeps the buoy from being sunk by the weight of what would be chain. If such a pennant is used it is important to be sure that eye splices are properly done and protective thimbles have been added. Much of the beneficial catenary (shock absorbing) effect of chain is lost in this situation. However, the stretch factor of the nylon makes up for some of this deficit.

Scope is an important concept. A good seaman realizes that more anchor rode is better than less. In today's crowded harbors, 2-1/2-to-1 ratios of length of mooring rode to depth of water is about all one can expect. This can be dangerous, especially in shallow water anchorages. It means that those moored in 10 feet of water with 25-foot chains may find themselves in a storm tide situation with 20 feet of water and only the 25-foot length of ground tackle. Add to this hurricane-force winds, and a grim picture takes shape. Those anchored in 40 feet of water are better off. They are tethered to a 100-foot rode, and the impact of a 10-foot storm tide would only change the ratio to 2-to-1. When a serious storm threatens, it's worth considering a means of extending the length of the mooring tether. Obviously, if swinging room is available, increased scope is a preferred option.

BUOYS AND PICK UP DEVICES

Your mooring buoy serves the important function of keeping the tackle from sinking to the bottom. There is no single answer to the question of which is the best type. I prefer an inflatable plastic ball that isn't as likely to damage a boat's topsides as it bumps against it in a calm sea. Unfortunately, these do seem to turn gummy after a couple of seasons and will smear the hull. Giving the buoy an occasional coat of linear polyurethane paint will remedy this problem.

Rather than practicing with a boathook, many boaters prefer what is called a tall-buoy pick up. The device has a flexible, fiberglass antenna-like whip that is weighted on one end and made buoyant with a cylindrical piece of Styrofoam placed a short distance above the weight. This vertical pick up is connected to the main mooring pennant by a short piece of nylon line. It makes

The hook connection between this mooring line and bow cleat is a fragile link at best.

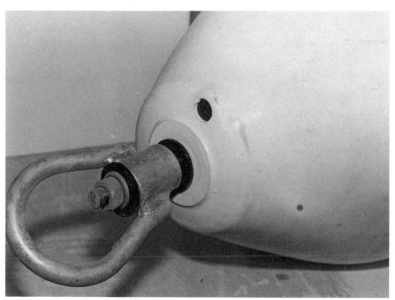

Beware of nuts that can loosen and hidden rods that can rust.

Chafe is an enemy of every moored boat.

retrieving the mooring on a windy, current-ridden day much less troublesome.

Some boat owners pull their mooring pennant line up on deck and affix it to a cleat. This can cause the line to be chafed at the point where the chock rubs on the line. Instead, I recommend a mooring bridle. This is basically a short piece (6 feet) of nylon with an eye splice on each end. Before the second splice is made, a piece of plastic tubing or PVC hose is pulled over the line. The bridle is slipped through the eye splice at the top of the pennant line, and each end is looped over a forward bow cleat. The bridle is not damaged through chafing and will usually afford several seasons of useful life. For additional chafe resistance, I use a plastic or galvanized thimble in the eye splice at the top of the pennant line.

In areas where there is prolific marine growth, a coat of antifouling paint on the upper part of the mooring unit is a distinct advantage. Prepare and paint buoys and nylon line in a conventional manner. If chain is to be painted, do not use a copper-based antifouling coating. Corrosion may develop between the

Left: *A well-sheathed mooring bridle significantly reduces chafe.* Right: *Close-up of mooring bridle, showing eyesplice and PVC hose.*

zinc galvanizing on the chain and the cuprous oxide in the paint. Normally chain only needs to be coated where it comes in close contact with the surface.

LOCATION MATTERS

Location is another vital mooring issue. Most developed harbors have municipally regulated mooring areas. It's a good idea to inquire about mooring regulations in a given location before purchasing any hardware. Some harbors require that all ground tackle be leased from one vendor, while others require a seasonal inspection of each set of ground tackle. In areas where moorings are grouped tightly in a controlled grid system, it is imperative that every boat be securely moored. It might not be a bad idea to test for yourself what the bottom conditions are like. This can be done with a small Danforth anchor or with a sounding lead to sample bottom sediment. Those who scuba dive may even want to take a look at the bottom and their neighbors' mooring anchors. In good holding ground, most of a heavy mushroom anchor should be buried. Beware of situations where all the anchors are perched on a hard, gravelly sea bed.

You may feel that all this concern is a bit excessive. However, you may change your mind halfway through the season's worst gale. In such conditions, moorings—yours as well as your neighbor's—are all that separate safety from disaster. Swinging room is usually limited, and even a small amount of dragging can result in one stern hammering against another bow. Overkill is the answer in such situations. It is the best way to be certain that your boat and those next to you stay where they belong.

In some areas, local ordinances allow you to put together your own mooring and set it yourself. No doubt there are dollars to be saved, but there are also additional responsibilities to be assumed. Focus on quality hardware as you gather the equipment required. New gear is costly, but may be the best buy in the long run. On the other hand, it's not hard to tell whether or not a used mushroom anchor is worth consideration. Corrosion damage is usually obvious. If you are able to purchase a secondhand anchor, in excellent condition, for about half the price of a new one, it is a worthwhile expenditure.

Chain can also be found at a bargain price, but there are a few complications involved. First, chain varies in more ways than just link diameter. Different alloys are used for different purposes. The higher the strength-to-weight ratio, the more expensive the product. Most domestic chain manufacturers recommend their proof coil, or "System 3," chain for standard mooring use. This chain has been tested by loading it to twice its recommended working load, and then every 20th length is inspected. BBB and High Tensile chain are even stronger, short-link alternatives, which tend to be more costly. There are many bargains available, but they vary greatly in quality. I prefer the products made by Campbell or American Chain and Cable Company. Strict government specifications necessitate a tightly controlled manufacturing process. Most bargains never seem to carry written specifications on the control process of their manufacture.

If you are considering a pile of used chain which seems in

Rusted chain can be the proverbial weak link in your ground tackle. Undersized or cheap chain is no bargain at any price.

good condition, look for the stamp of the manufacturer. This usually occurs on a link every foot or so. If you determine the chain comes from a reputable supplier and it hasn't sustained link-stretching overloads or excessive corrosion, it may be a bargain after all. Just to be on the safe side, you may want to consider only secondhand chain that is one size larger than what the specs call for.

LAUNCHING YOUR MOORING

Placing a mooring is not quite as simple as it seems. If you plan to do it all yourself, be sure you have the blessings of the local town fathers, and make sure you have met all the bureaucratic constraints involved. If permits are required and an inspection mandated, meet the requirements, then launch your mooring. Finding out at a later date that your mooring is illegal and must be pulled won't add any pleasure to the sailing season.

If you have another person to help you, a convenient way to launch a mooring is to load it on the deck of a small float and tow it to the desired location. A pair of 55-gallon oil drums securely lashed together and supporting an upper platform may do the trick, but it's vital that the float be stable enough to support a person, and to allow the weight of the anchor and ground tackle to be shifted to the edge prior to launching. As you tow this makeshift barge into position, be sure that the mushroom is inboard enough and lashed to prevent unintentional launching, and that the chain has been carefully flaked out on deck. Maneuver the float to the location desired, keeping in mind how far astern the scope will reach out, and considering the consequences of swinging room. Just before you make the drop, double check the shackles to make sure they have a secondary means of keeping the clevis pins from turning. If all seems in order, ease the mushroom anchor off the edge of the float, making very sure that you are well away from the chain as it follows the anchor to the bottom. Once the mooring is on the bottom, pull the tackle in the same direction that your boat will likely stream in most bad weather situations. This straightens out the chain and also tips over the anchor shank, lessening the chance of having the rode inadvertently wrap around it. Power hard against the pull of the tackle in order to set the anchor. Obviously, this operation requires good timing and careful coordination between the person in the towing boat and the person on the float. Safety should be of paramount concern. Several fathoms of chain whipping overboard behind a hefty mushroom anchor are a potentially lethal weapon.

Most boaters prefer to have their moorings hauled by a crew specializing in such services. However, the ardent do-it-yourselfer has a few other options. The tide can be as effective as the most powerful winch. All it takes to haul your own mooring is a float or a few 55-gallon drums, some heavy line, and the patience to allow the tide to do its work. Rig the float to a taut mooring rode at low water, and later, as the tide rises, the anchor will be pulled clear of the bottom. At high water move the suspended tackle into water shallow enough for the anchor to again touch. Repeat the process as often as necessary in order to reach the shore. Spring tides, with their larger range between high and low water, offer the best opportunity. Be sure that the flotation device you use is appropriate for the given weight of the tackle involved. This is an effective but tedious process; as mentioned earlier, most owners prefer to hire someone with a powerful winch or crane to do their mooring hauling.

Appendix • Quality Operations

THERE ARE SUBTLE differences among top quality boat-yards and marinas. While in the process of writing this book, I visited a wide variety of facilities and had a chance to see various approaches to handling the needs of boat owners. This section of the book looks at several examples of successful service operations and the particular characteristics that add to their effectiveness. It is a description, not a directory; its purpose is to help boat owners become better aware of their own priorities, and the range of options available, when choosing a boatyard or a marina. Customer satisfaction is the common factor that ties the majority of these diverse operations together. Each seems to accomplish this welcome result despite differing methodologies.

Essex Boatworks, in Essex, Connecticut, is a full-service boatyard worth a close look. Owner Stu Ingersoll has been careful to keep his staff in touch with current technology as well as with traditional craftsmanship. His employees can do metal fabrication, wooden boat refits, and engine rebuilds; they can also handle the most sophisticated of sprayable plastic coatings. His clients are looking for full marine maintenance service and inside winter storage. They aren't do-it-yourself oriented folks, and their requirements keep a staff of 20 or so employees busy during the cold winter months. A walk through this mid-sized facility shows a boat owner how things should be done. Yes, this type of maintenance is costly, but boat owners who value top quality work and are willing to pay for it will not be disappointed by the results at Essex Boatworks.

The facility occupies a strategic corner of the Essex waterfront. Land is limited, and the operation has optimized its productivity through effective boat handling. Vessels are hauled out of the water with either a conventional travelift or an old but well-maintained Algonac Hoist, a sling lift which runs on a marine railway track. Since storage room is at a premium and travelift placement requires more distance between boats, each vessel is placed in a steel cradle and towed by a hydraulic Kleeco trailer to a tightly organized location inside a large shed. This double handling allows for effective use of all available space.

Stu Ingersoll has also adopted an innovative approach to management. He was an early leader in data processing, as well as an advocate of merit pay. The gainsharing plan he put into effect provides employees with a monthly financial bonus for productivity above the norm. He rewards those who develop multiple job skills and involve themselves in appropriate training programs. This type of outlook benefits both the individual and the business.

Just down the Connecticut Shoreline, southwest of Essex, lies **Pilot's Point Marina.** The boatyard is one of a chain of facilities owned by Jack Brewer and is run by a talented sailor and manager, Rives Potts. The yard is an engineering feat, which has grown out of a marshy bog. Over the years it has been developed section by section into a mammoth facility. The large amount of available land permits outside dry storage and also allows for plenty of parking for boat owners using the slips during the summer months. There is also inside storage, as well as shop facilities—both accommodated in prefab metal buildings. A new travelift slipway features two separate bay arrangements to handle lifts of various sizes. The spar unstepping crane and rigging area are adjacent to the travelift pier. Just beyond this active portion of the yard are a new office complex and spray shed facility. The yard also maintains a primitive but effective keel casting foundry, providing foiled ballast for IOR boats and meter boats. The most competitive sailors find keel and rudder swaps to be a regular part of an IOR facelift. Pilot's Point finds that such services benefit clients and help keep craftsmen busy during the long winter months. Innovative thinking keeps such facilities flexible enough to stay current with yachting needs.

The **Henry R. Hinckley** yard, in Southwest Harbor, Maine, is a boatbuilding operation with an associated service yard, and has a reputation for excellence built upon action rather than advertising. Since so much is going on in the building and refit aspects of the operation, some people are surprised to find the famous Hinckley attention to detail equally prevalent at the transient docks. The operation is well staffed, and great efforts are made to accommodate the steady, summer-long parade of cruising sailors. Repair charges are not in the bargain basement price range, but the work is first rate, and the effort to accommodate each situation is laudable. I recall poking about the yard and having a chat with a sailor whose fuel-injection pump on his Pathfinder diesel had given up the ghost. There were no dealers in the area, but the Hinckley staff finally traced down a pump at a nearby Volkswagen dealer. Since the Pathfinder Marine engine starts life as a VW, it was a creative place to look for the part. As soon as the part was received, a mechanic was on hand to do the installation, and the sailor was cruising again with only a slight delay. Service like this to cruising yachtsmen helps a yard's reputation immensely.

Yacht Haven Inc., in Stamford, Connecticut, is the largest service yard in the East, with storage facilities for some six or seven hundred boats on land, and a growing winter wet storage fleet. Its floating marinas are filled to capacity during the summer months. This high-density boating population has attracted a variety of specialized services. The yard itself runs a comprehensive operation, providing services ranging from mechanical work to spray painting. In addition, there are associated businesses, including a rigging loft, a complete electronics facility, and a chandlery right on the premises.

Yacht Haven's size has also resulted in some pioneering achievements in the data processing field. President Lee Frantz Jr.

took the experience gained from computerizing the operation and put together a software package called Sextant Systems, which tracks a work order from the employee's time card to the final, automatically compiled, customer statement. The package not only streamlines the billing process, but can provide spreadsheets, which give the yard administration information on employee productivity, input on seasonal profit fluctuations, and other handy management tools. Storage contracts and slip rentals are also stored in the data base.

When the 98-foot motorsailer *Anadarko* broke her 110-foot box section spruce spar in the Caribbean, a replacement wasn't easy to find. **Wayfarer Marine Corporation,** in Camden, Maine, decided to take on the challenge. The carpenters' first project was to construct a spar bench long enough to act as a gluing platform for the hefty mast, but once the logistics were in place the project proceeded without major problems. When the epoxy glue had cured and the varnish coats had dried, *Anadarko's* new main mast was ready for stepping. This is another example of the diversity found in many topnotch yards. Yards like Wayfarer, which keep traditional boatbuilding skills alive and occasionally are able to capitalize on the fact that they are doing so, serve more than their own needs. They create a means of passing on skills too easily forgotten. The day may not be too far off where those who want to see a wooden spar being built will have to go to the Mystic Seaport Museum, to a spar bench next to the cooper's shed.

Cove Haven, in Barrington, Rhode Island, is a full-service, high-tech facility. A 150-ton travelift provides considerable hauling capacity. It's not unusual to see barges and workboats hauled and painted in this predominantly yacht-oriented boatyard. In other facilities this has proven to be a dangerous mixture because the sandblasting involved in repainting metal boats sends clouds of gritty dust flying everywhere, and yacht owners look for other storage options. But the crew at Cove Haven is meticulous about confining the abrasive grit to where it is being used. The extra time spent containing the potential aggravation is offset by the good will this generates among the yard's clients.

Cove Haven's refit and painting reputation has attracted many 12-meter boats—at least while the Cup was still being sailed for in local waters. The last time I visited the yard the spray paint crew was about ready to spray a larger Berger motor yacht. The prime coats and prep work held up to close scrutiny. The final coats of LPU paint were applied by a team of spray painters. Three men worked in unison to keep a wet edge and even flow pattern on the massive topsides. The results of their efforts are the best I have seen anywhere. The Cove Haven painters demonstrate how quality comes from attention to detail. They maintain an organized approach, learning from setbacks as well as accomplishments, and over the years they have continued to refine their talents. As modern painting technology has evolved, they have evolved right along with it.

West Shore Marina, in Huntington, New York, represents a growing trend in the Northeast toward full-service, floating dock marinas. At West Shore there is a fixed pier with ramps and floating docks radiating out into the bay. Water, electricity, and telephone service are all available, and an Acme Lift and a crane are on hand for hauling service and repairs. The marina has a chandlery and a nicely landscaped location.

Operations such as this have long been commonplace in the West and the South, where there is a year-round boating climate, but they are recent arrivals in the Northeast. In the past, the cost of pile driving and dock building could not easily be offset by what summer storage rates generated. But today those rates have risen, and the growing popularity of winter wet storage has made year-round utilization an increasingly viable option. A number of marina owners have installed anti-ice systems, and many of their clients' boats remain tied to slips over the winter, using the yard's hauling equipment at off-peak times for a quick coat of bottom paint. This adds revenue, helping to offset the initial capital investment.

Like other successful marinas, West Shore provides a quality facility and aims for full utilization. From the outset, there was a commitment to sound construction; the pier was designed with ice and winter northerlies in mind. In addition to a sound structural approach, the designers kept a total use pattern in mind. Once the dockside facilities were completed, Phase Two of the building program went into effect. An architecturally pleasing office and chandlery building was constructed, parking facilities were laid out, and the entire location was landscaped.

Skeptics in the area felt that half the slips would remain empty for years. But even before construction was complete, customers began to flock to the new facility, and within months the marina was filled. In the Northeast, dockside locations for boats are still well behind the demand—one of the few parts of the current boating industry that is in a steep growth phase.

At **Zahniser's Marina and Boatyard** in Solomons Island, Maryland, the management has chosen to stress aesthetic factors, and the facility has an attractive, Mystic Seaport Museum atmosphere. The concentration on ambience hasn't hindered the quality of the workmanship. Skilled craftsmen, taking pride in their trade as well as in the yard's image, continue to please their customers. At Zahniser's, an absence of clutter and a community of carefully painted shops and offices send a message to all who enter the yard. Customers rightfully assume that if the staff pays such attention to the detail of their surroundings, they will take the same approach with the boats they service. Zahniser's stands behind its image—a very first class yacht facility.

Across the Chesapeake, on the Eastern Shore, lies the sleepy Sassafrass River. Located at the head of this river is **Georgetown Yacht Services.** Phil Parish runs a very complete marine facility, handling anything from bottom blister repairs to the installation of masthead antennas. The operation provides several hundred slips for local as well as transient boaters. Like so many other regional facilities, Georgetown Yacht Services has discovered a seasonal rhythm to its service operation. The Chesapeake Bay is a migratory route for more than waterfowl, and each spring and fall, Georgetown Yacht Services sees its fair share of cruising sailors in need of repair work. Phil Parish feels that the transient is looking for fast, effective repairs, and he and his staff do all in their power to provide them. There is a refrigeration specialist on staff, and parts on hand to solve most of the common maladies. The facility also specializes in major refits and long-term storage—not just winter storage, either. Many owners who take their boats south for the winter choose to leave them at Georgetown Yacht Services for summer storage and any refit maintenance necessary. Here, again, is a good example of how alertness to a specific regional need can enhance a yard's productivity.

A bit farther south on the coastal migratory route lies **Atlantic Yacht Basin,** in Great Bridge, Virginia. Business has been helped by its location at one of the busiest points on the Intracoastal Waterway. Passagemakers headed north or south can tie alongside a bulkhead and arrange anything from a diesel fuel fill-up to a complete refit. The marina has slips available, and a very well-staffed mechanical department. The on-site store stocks many engine parts, and prices tend to be better than those in chandleries north or south of the area. The folks who run this operation have been able to maintain a friendly as well as helpful attitude toward waterway migrants. This, in itself, is getting to be an endangered outlook. A small marina a bit to the south has a prominent sign on the floating dock which proclaims: "PAY FIRST THEN ASK QUESTIONS."

The **Municipal Marinas** in Annapolis, Maryland; Charlestown, South Carolina; and St. Augustine, Florida are town-owned facilities that wave a welcome sign to those in transit along the Intracoastal Waterway. Wise town fathers have seen fit to offer the voyager a chance to tie up, take a shower, and wander through the heart of these waterfront communities. Most visitors aren't looking for haulouts and complex refits, nor are these facilities equipped to handle such needs, but there are mechanics, electricians, and other in-the-water marine services on hand. Although quite a few of the slips available at these facilities see a new vessel every few days, there are also numerous full-time residents, as well as a sizable percentage of long-term visitors, staying for the entire season.

David Lowe's Boatyard and Marina in Stuart, Florida, is the right place to find a cost-effective refit and a quiet stay away from the bustling tourist scene. Lowe runs a first class marine operation, featuring three new travelifts and some of the best brush painters to be found anywhere. The boatyard is a clean, well-organized facility, and over the years expansion has been slow and deliberate, with an unwavering commitment to quality and productivity.

A bit farther north along the Intracoastal Waterway lies a do-it-yourself haven called **Cracker Brothers Boatyard.** It is a no-frills bargain featuring good haulout equipment. Those with their own tools and skills will have a chance to tinker, grind, varnish, and polish to their hearts' content. There is neither clubhouse, restaurant, nor squash courts, and proper yachting attire usually means shorts and a T-shirt. Cracker Brothers is home to a clientele of hardy, self-reliant folks who maintain their boats themselves, save money, and go cruising. Certainly this option is not for everybody, but for those who have learned to tackle their own boating refit needs, yards such as Cracker Brothers afford a money-saving alternative to the full-service boatyard.

Irish Boat Shop in Harbor Springs, Michigan, is as full service a marine facility as any of its saltwater cousins. The business is composed of two yards: a floating slip marina and a shoreside operation that includes a yacht brokerage and a sail loft. Irish Boat Shop has one of the best spray booth facilities in the area and is well known for quality Awlgrip and Imron work. Their 250-slip marina includes fuel dock facilities and a waste pump-out station.

Like most facilities on the Great Lakes, Irish Boat Shop faces a rather short boating season. From mid-May to early September customers make the most of the boating season. The boat shop staff swells to about 60 during the busy part of the season; a smaller contingent of craftsmen works year round on refit and maintenance projects. In addition to a travelift and hydraulic cranes, Irish

Ondine *undergoing a major refit at the Kettenberg Yard, Channel Islands Harbor, California.*

Boat Shop also has a 40-ton Hawk hydraulic trailer, used for both in-yard and over-the-road boat transport. The operation stores about 700 boats during the winter months.

The **Kettenberg Yard,** in Channel Islands Harbor, California, is a large yard with a respected reputation in boatbuilding and major refit work. Ten years ago I watched the yard do a major and innovative overhaul on Sumner Long's maxi boat *Ondine.* The day after she was powered into the Kettenberg slipway, her spars were out and a metal worker had cut the last 10 feet off her stern. By the following week an entirely new stern was welded in place. During that same week the paint crew was increasing the girth of the boat's underwater forward section by troweling on a massive amount of an epoxy microballoon mixture, bonded to alloy stringers that had been welded to the outer hull skin. These efforts to gain a couple of tenths of a knot of racing speed were labor intensive but superbly orchestrated. Sometimes it takes seeing what a large yard can do to put smaller projects in perspective.

Not far from the Kettenberg Yard, the **Channel Islands Harbor Marina** is representative of a number of municipal marinas along the California coast. This is a modern, well-planned facility, serving a year-round boating population. Marina businesses are leased from the town, and the number of slips is tightly controlled by the municipal government. Each vessel has its own U-shaped berth, with floating finger docks on each side of the boat. Ashore, there are shower facilities and a laundromat not far from the head of the gangway. A ship's chandlery and numerous restaurants are within walking distance.

Index